DIVINE
by
NATURE

www.michellehankes.com

ANGEL GIRL PUBLICATIONS

Divine by Nature

Spiritual Messages from the Planet's
Natural Elements

Michelle L. Hankes

For my mom

The problem with humans is we think we're ingenious alone.

Ingenious, we are; alone, we are not.

There is a way that nature speaks, that land speaks. Most of the time we are simply not patient enough, quiet enough, to pay attention to the story.

- Linda Hogan

Table of Contents

Every blade of grass has its angel that bends over it and whispers, "Grow, grow."

- The Talmud

INTRODUCTION

Imagine walking through a forest. You see rocks and trees, clouds high up in the sky, and birds flittering by overhead. You might see raindrops or dewdrops hanging from tree branches, and moss or lichen slowing crawling its way up the side of a fallen tree. There may be bugs and insects buzzing past you on a journey into the depths of the forest, searching out food or companionship, or maybe even a noontime human meal. The air might be palpable with tinges of moisture, the smell of mildew hovering above the freshly-wet ground, and a squirrel skittering across the treetops in search of something more than the passerby strolling beneath.

As you stop and look around, what more do you see? Do you see the life living in this brown and green enviroscape as nothing more than a bunch of plants and animals and green things? Or do you see something beyond - something deeper within the forest that makes you want to know more? *Is there more to life than just what we see?*

Life is made up of nothing more than energy in neatly, or not so neatly, arranged patterns. Every living and inanimate thing is just tightly woven energy that we see with our eyes, sense with our senses, and touch with our skin. But what about that which we cannot see? What about that which animates the inanimate and brings life to the plants and animals and trees? What is this so-called life that brings life alive?

Have you ever looked at a rock or a tree and seen a face staring back at you? Did you ever look up at the clouds and see an image carved across the sky with perfect precision wondering if it wasn't just by chance? Have you ever wondered why plants that are talked to and sung to grow faster, bigger, and respond better than plants that are ignored? For one simple reason: because there is life in everything. And not just the life you see before you. It is the life *within* these things that really matters. I'm not only talking about the cells and structures and mechanisms that bring something to life in the physical way we know, but what about the life beyond life? What is it that drives and creates and manifests life into life? What's really behind what we see?

Life is about the energy that runs through all things in our Universe, the creative force behind it, and the individual nature of everything.

On the most basic level, everything is nothing more than energy. Thoughts, bodies, water, air – everything. Energy is what makes things into things and all energy is the same, coming from the same Universal source just in uniquely variant patterns. It can never be destroyed, only transformed into something else, some other pattern. And the energy that is manifested into things is exchanged into various forms by vibration. It is the different vibrations that allow physical life to exist by letting the energy vibrate in different patterns that we eventually see as something physical.

But beyond the energy that creates something physically, there is a more precious energy – an individual, infinite energy and vibration that creates a uniqueness; an individuation from everything else - the individuation from the whole. Some call this individual vibration spirit, soul, essence, or beingness. It doesn't matter what you call it: what matters is that *it does exist in all things*. We each have universal life in us creating and nourishing us, yet something separates me from you and you from me. This is our individual soul creating its own life experience. And everything has a soul. Trees, rocks, plants, clouds, wind, water, earth, and sky. No exceptions. Just as we, as human beings, have life within us, all things, *living or inanimate*, have life as well.

Now, the energy that permeates physical bodies is really no different than the energy that runs through our beings that creates our individuality. And in broader terms, the very same energy that creates our physical bodies and our individual souls is the energy that animates the entire Universe. All of these energies are one and the same, but the difference is the uniqueness of expression. The energy that permeates all of us and everything is expressing itself as your individual creation, my individual creation and the individual creations of millions and millions of other things – the shrubs, the rivers, the rain, the birds, the flowers, the mountains, the oceans and even the Earth itself. We are all connected and yet, we are all expressing ourselves in our own unique way. That is the beauty of the Universe – the ability to be connected to All That Is and still be who we choose to be. And on planet Earth, this individual expression is being expressed by millions and millions of entities living their own lives, creating their own truths, and being their Divine selves here in a physical body. Humans, animals, nature – all creating within the space of the Divine and learning to live with one another. It's a magnificent opportunity and we are all on this journey together. Just as we are spiritual beings having a human experience, all around us are spiritual beings having their own physical experiences in the different forms of nature. Life exists everywhere, not just in some things, but in *all things*.

Life is meant to be lived in many different forms and it is this uniqueness that allows the expression of the Whole to be more palpable.

There are an infinite number of non-physical (spiritual) beings on Planet Earth - some inhabiting a physical form and some not - each with multiple purposes and many wanting to befriend and help those who want to connect with them. They have knowledge of this Earth and the Universe that we are only just beginning to understand in the human race. Many of them have been here long before we ever set foot upon this planet and they will be here long after. Many of you already know about spirit guides, ancestral helpers, Angels, Archangels, animal totems, fairies, elementals, dragons, and devas, and many of you already connect with them in your own personal way. Yet there is a vast multitude of other beings connected to us wanting to communicate and offer their wisdom. Just as we express our own brand of truth, so do all of these other entities and it may be their truth that helps guide you to your own.

Consciousness exists in many, many forms and it is this consciousness that gives life to the physical bodies we see all around us. For every physical body you see, there is a non-physical being attached to it, guiding it and expressing its own brand of creative manifestation. There is a being attached to literally everything - your body, your house, bodies of water, this book. There are also beings for every thought, idea, concept, and creation as well. And even more infinitely beyond that. There are beings that watch, oversee, direct, guide, engage in and enjoy the experience of whatever they have created, tangible or intangible. We interact with these beings all the time, only most of us don't recognize them as such. They are engaged in their own kind of experience here on Earth and we have learned to block them out of our awareness. Children and animals display an immense ability to pick up on the non-physical beings around them because the ability hasn't been taught out of them. Not only do children and animals connect with ghosts or Angels, but nature beings as well. Many children have seen and worked with fairies, gnomes, sprites, brownies, and pixies and they are highly sensitive to the spiritual energies of plants, trees and other nature entities. They see what we have forgotten to continue seeing.

Nature beings are expansive, just as expansive as the natural world. There are spiritual beings associated with each blade of grass, each pebble of sand, each drop of rain, as well as the entirety of the Earth itself. And we are capable of communicating and connecting with each and every one of them. They can help us with our own experience here on Earth, making it better, more fulfilled and more connected to the source of energy that is everything, as well as helping us to express our individual creative desires.

The creatures that inhabit this earth - be they human beings or animals - are here to contribute, each in its own particular way, to the beauty and prosperity of the world.

- Dalai Lama

Humans have been communicating and working with nature since the beginning of history. Ancient societies lived within the natural world, but modern societies have to work more to connect and stay in-tune. Having an outdoor space to connect with nature helps, but nature can live indoors with us too. Talk to your plants, your flowers, your herbs. They all have consciousness and they want to communicate with you. How do you think ancient societies knew which plant helped particular infirmities? The plants and people were connected. They communicated with one another in ways we have since forgotten, but with a little practice and patience, your inherent nature will come shining through.

Your work is to discover your world and then with all your heart, give yourself to it.

- Buddha

DIVINE NATURE

As it is with each individual human being, each entity of nature is experiencing its own existence, its own purpose, and its own vibrational voice. They each have a unique personality, just as we do. They all have their own expression and life experiences they are pursuing. I have found in my work with the various nature beings that there are those who want to help, those who just want to communicate or connect, and those who want to be left alone, just like the varied kinds of people and animals we all know. Some are eager and welcome the chance to connect, while others do not want to be touched or communicated with. Every being has its own desires for creation and how it wants to express itself - and sometimes those desires and expressions change.

A good example is the three trees that live near my driveway that love to connect with me. These three sister tree beings (as I call them) chose an existence knowing it would include people and lots of them, for a very long period of time. They have seen many people come and go and build things around them, as well as watch and experience the existence of numerous plants, flowers, insects, and other beings. They are happy, loving trees enjoying their existence in this moment - until recently. Over the past couple of years, one of the trees has expressed a strong energetic desire to no longer be communicated with, touched or intruded upon in any way. I have taken note of this request without fully knowing the reason or desire behind it because I have such great respect for these three trees and their experiences. The other two trees are still quite eager to connect with me and readily grant permission for tree hugs and energy exchanges. Just as with people, things change. One of the tree sisters is making a desired choice for her own experience, just as I am making one for mine: to honor her.

I have taken walks in urban and remote areas and encountered unhappy nature beings - amongst equally happy ones - who did not want to communicate, they did not want to engage, nor were they having what we would call "a pleasant experience." Sometimes, their roots were rotting and aching with disease. Other ones I have seen are filled with insect infestations eating away at their core. It doesn't matter what kind of experience they are having because for us to judge that it is not the right kind of experience places our truth on them. The truth is we do not know what they are here to experience and if they want our help, they will ask for it. Most of the time, these nature beings and their energies are not harmful, but the energy surrounding them tends to not be inviting and it would be disrespectful for us to intrude on their experience the way they have chosen it. There is also the possibility of allowing the negative energy from their experience into our own lives. If they ask for assistance energetically or physically, that's a whole other matter, which we will get into in the next chapter. Either way, honoring one another - *no matter the type of being or the experience* - will not only benefit you, but it will benefit the Whole as well.

Today, more than ever before, life must be characterized by a sense of Universal responsibility, not only nation to nation and human to human, but also human to other forms of life.

- Dalai Lama

Be Mindful of Your Energy and Your Actions

In cases previously described, and in all cases really, I communicate with each being and ask permission to talk, touch or connect with it, just as you would another person. Hopefully, you would not walk right up to someone and just accost them, verbally or physically. You would begin with an energy introduction. Engaging with nature is not much different than engaging with other people or any other being, for that matter. Be aware and mindful of your own energy and your own actions. Many times, we do things and we don't even realize that we've done something. I've seen people standing by a tree and picking off leaves, branches and bark as though it didn't mean anything to anyone. I can assure you, it does. Be aware of what you are doing and what your actions may be doing to the other entities around you. Would you enjoy someone walking up to you and pulling hairs off your head or picking off pieces of your skin? Probably not. Not to mention all the other little entities living on those trees and inside them. Bugs, insects, microbes, and fungi all live symbiotically (most of the time) with trees and other plants. Pulling off pieces of their home is akin to a big tree falling on your house or someone ripping off some siding. Be aware of where you place your body, your hands and your fingers. According to the nature entities, this reminder is not about the pain it may cause them - this is about respect for one another. Be mindful of what you are doing and who you are doing it to – your actions do have an effect, whether you realize it or not.

If the nature being welcomes an opportunity to connect with you, then pursue it, and if not, respect the being's wishes and move on. Why not find someone who wants to talk and be with you? That is much more pleasant for everyone involved. You will have a more connected experience this way and so will they. And if their intention and yours is to gain assistance, the offering you both will get will be much richer and rewarding.

Keep in mind too, that if you ask a nature being to talk with you and they decline or you get no response at all, it could be a temporary situation. You can always try again later or just simply let them know they can come to you if they would ever like to have an experience with you. I have had beings visit me after I had first met them having expressed to them they are welcome to come at a later time and engage with me. Moonbeam beings, fairies, and a few other beings typically work this way because they want to really see something in you before they engage in a communicative relationship. However, once they do, it can last a lifetime.

We are all travelers in the wilderness of this world, and the best that we can find in our travels is an honest friend.
- Robert Louis Stevenson

Most nature beings are working towards creating some physical experience (souls moving towards gaining a physical body), which will turn into a physical existence (being in the body), and eventually, a new physical creation (creating within the body, physical manifestations around the body, physical experiences, or creating new life). As they are experiencing their chosen creation, some beings prefer a sole experience, others prefer to work as individuals in a group and still others desire to become unified homogeneously in a group. Any combination is possible and once you begin to explore and experience these connections, you will see the multitude of possibilities for different types and ways of experiencing life.

Trees are a great example: some tree beings prefer an individual experience, yet they cluster in groups around a specific area. You see this often times in a forest with lots of individual trees all clumped together or huddled together in a park. You might be surprised to realize that this is more their doing and their chosen experience rather than what we think humans have done to them.

Other times you will find one solitary tree in a field somewhere. This is an individual, sole type of experience, but the tree is hardly alone. There could be all sorts of other nature beings in the tree's experience including water beings, rock beings, grass or plant beings, human beings and more. Even if you think you're alone, you never really are.

I have also met trees, often very old trees, that are a conglomerate of several tree beings acting as one unified whole to create one or more physical trees. Many times, you will see trees like this with what seem to be lots of faces (and they are) staring back at you from one trunk. Another example is a grouping of trees that is growing out of the same trunk or root system. There is an infinite variety of ways to experience whatever creation is being created. Sometimes you just need to connect and experience the beings to recognize which type they are. And truthfully, the type doesn't really matter - the desire to connect does. Focus on that and you'll definitely meet some fascinating trees.

Rocks work in much the same way. There are many, many rock beings found on beaches, most working as individuals in a group situation. Other times, you will drive along an open stretch of highway and find a huge rock completely by itself out in a pasture. This rock could be having a singular rock experience, or it may prefer to engage with other beings besides rock beings, or there is more than one non-physical being associated with that rock in the form of a group dynamic. There are so many possibilities and so many ways to experience the art of creation and this will become more and more apparent as you watch the nature beings creating their worlds within our one world.

There is only one success – to be able to spend your life in your own way.

- Christopher Morley

Each nature being, as with human beings, is unique in that it has chosen a particular life path to experience itself and its existence. In choosing a particular pathway, each being demonstrates a choice regarding its motives about experiencing something new or the same. This regard allows it to maintain its individuality without sacrificing its need to exist simultaneously with other beings. This leads to a particular individual or group existence.

Many people wonder if nature beings live physically within their creation or reside outside it. Just as with other non-physical entities, including human and animal souls, some nature beings fully inhabit their physicalness and take on the characteristics of their type of nature. This is when you can see faces in rocks, trees, and in the sky. Others just stay near their physical body and morph the physical body to look as they choose it to. Some may be surprised to know that people do the same thing. There are human beings who become very engaged and entwined with their physical creation, inhabiting it and really experiencing the fullness of physical existence. Still there are others who prefer a less physical approach to their experience and work from outside their creation, which allows them to experience a physical experience without having to become as deeply engaged as those who inhabit their creation.

Why would this be so? Simply because it is a different type of experience and a different way to experience oneself and the Whole. Since we all co-exist with physical bodies more than once throughout our soul's journeys, we choose something different with each experience to gain a new perspective. You will always choose to be human in your experiences here on Earth, but in each life, you are someone new. Nature is no different. For some of them, their lives are shorter than a human life. For many, their lives are considerably longer. But each time, we all get to choose again to create something new. That's the fun in being with a physical body! I have found some patterns among different types of nature in what they might choose, how they might choose it, or even that a species as a whole tends to have a similar mission, but it still comes down to an individual choice and an individual experience, so I suggest you communicate with as many nature beings as you want and see what you see for yourself.

In our universe we are tuned into the frequency that corresponds to physical reality. But there are an infinite number of parallel realities coexisting with us in the same room, although we cannot tune into them.

— Steven Weinberg,
Nobel Prize-winning
Quantum Physicist

Masculine or Feminine?

You will notice as you engage with different aspects of nature, they may come across with a specific feeling of masculine or feminine energy or sometimes neutral, meaning a little of both or really no specific energetic pattern at all. As I describe my encounters in the upcoming chapters, I have chosen to use terms such as 'he' and 'she' for descriptive purposes. Keep in mind that these beings do not carry a gender; not as we know it in human form. They are not male and female. However, in many instances, they do exude a generalization of masculine or feminine energy, just as we humans do. For these types of energy, I use he/she for simplicity once I've described the energy that I experienced. The type of energy they exude is important, just as it is for humans, because it characterizes the work and chosen experience.

The Universe is all about balance – balance of energy, balance of duality, balance of life systems. It is important that all energy be balanced to function properly within our dual nature here on Earth as well. Most beings exude some proportion of both energies and this will fluctuate over the experience. Sometimes a non-physical being will use multiple types of energy for varied purposes based on what they are experiencing or what they are doing in that moment. They may also change their predominant energy throughout their life to match new experiences or changes in what they are choosing. If you are having trouble understanding this or relating to it, think about yourself. Even though you probably exude a predominant type of energy (masculine or feminine), you also work with the opposite to balance yourself. We are working with both energies all the time in any given situation, as do the nature beings, well beyond our physical emanation through our body's gender. We are giving and receiving, healing and breaking down, creating and reabsorbing all the time on many, many different levels. The energy and life forms around you are no different, except in their choices. When a being is finally able to fully maintain an even exchange of both energies at the same time, all the time, their energy will begin to feel neutral. It becomes a perfect blend as we become closer to being energetically balanced.

Feminine energy tends to be about receiving and healing oneself, whereas masculine energy tends to about giving, healing others, and caretaking as needed. Male energy provides relief from outside source intrusions. Feminine energy is about nurturing the self and allowing the self to receive from other sources to resupply and rejuvenate diminished energy patterns. Male energy is the energy that does the supplying and mends energy patterns that have gone askew. The two balance all energy patterns and are required for energetic harmony. Thus, when nature beings use a specific type of energy, or combinations in specific patterns, there is meaning behind why they are exuding a particular type. The energy is not truly masculine or feminine; it is simply energy that feels a certain way that we have come to understand as male or female energy. These terms are simply descriptors and not about gender, as nature beings do not exude gender like we do. Most beings prefer a certain type of energy while they conduct their projected physical creation, although they may take on different energy patterns at different times.

The type of energy we are all projecting is important, not the terminology. Please keep this in mind as you are reading my descriptions and if you get hung up on the male/female verbiage, substitute your own description or simply call them non-physicals as you read along.

A person connecting with nature is as easy as taking a walk in the woods.

There are so many nature beings in various forms to communicate with and we all have the capacity and ability to connect with any or all of them. Nature beings are excellent beings to begin your non-physical communication. For those who already communicate with non-physicals like spirit guides, elementals, or Angels, this will come easily and naturally. For those who are just beginning, but have often felt a deep connection with nature, this will also be easy for you. Just keep practicing and spending time with nature. Open yourself, open your own beingness to All That Is and trust what you see, hear, feel or experience. And the more you do it, the more you will experience wondrous creations in many varied places, places you could never have even imagined.

It takes two to speak the truth – one to speak and another to hear.

- Henry David Thoreau

HOW TO COMMUNICATE WITH NATURE

Working with nature beings is simple and easy. Anyone can do it as long as you are patient with yourself, take the time to connect with who you are and where you are, and just be in your environment. Nature beings are highly adept at communicating with people and they are eager to share their knowledge and experiences. Choose a pleasurable place to sit and enjoy nature or engage with your favorite patch of land.

To begin working with nature beings, start by spending time in nature. Nature is readily accessible to most of us and for those in shorter supply, nature can be brought into the home. Take the time and patience to sit with or within nature and truly experience what nature has to offer. Nature can be anything from a forested trail to a city park to sitting with your houseplants or in your backyard. If you have beach access, go there. If there is a local lake or nature trail, find a place that is comfortable for you and venture there. To open up the world of the nature beings to you, it doesn't have to be a big amount of nature. Whatever makes you feel comfortable and at ease, that is the best plan for you. I know instances where nature beings are profoundly and readily accessible simply by opening up to air beings or cloud beings. It doesn't have to be a tree or earth. Nature is truly everywhere and so are the nature beings.

Once you find a place and a moment to truly engage with nature, just sit with it and be in it. Enter into spiritual communion with nature by feeling yourself in nature and nature in yourself. Our molecules are one and the same. Engage in that. Entice it by inviting it in and taking your self out. Enter into nature as an experience of the Oneself and allow it to experience you as you experience it.

Our task must be to free ourselves from this prison by widening our circle of compassion to embrace all living creatures and the whole of nature and its beauty.

– Albert Einstein

What does all that mean? It can mean many things, *anything*, depending on what you want or need it to mean. Nature can be experienced in a myriad of ways. You can just sit with it and breathe it in. You can hold nature in your hands and feel its experience. You can stimulate your mind and your eyes by looking at it and really seeing it. You can smell the sweet, pungent, natural smells of nature and fill your senses in lots of different ways. You can listen to the sounds of nature and the world around you and allow the sounds to vibrate within your cells. You can experience your oneness by allowing nature to fill you and your essence to become nature. Nature is abundantly available in so many ways and can be experienced in any way you choose.

Once you begin to understand your connection to nature on a cellular and energetic level, you can begin to open your mind to the nature beings. You cannot experience them if you do not even acknowledge their physical bodies. This is simply the easiest way to begin a nature conversation.

When you have taken the presence of nature into your being, allow your mind to wonder about it. What is it like to be a tree? What does it feel like to grow as grass does? Why does rain make us feel good? Why does that one flower grow there instead of next to all the others? These questions will allow you to proclaim an interest in who they are and why they do what they do. Nature beings enjoy communication, but only with those who really seek their companionship. Invading their domain is not conducive to a respectable relationship. Think of it in terms of walking up to someone on the street. If you are respectful and courteous of their beingness, they are most likely going to respond favorably to you. If you dominate them or attempt to intrude upon their space, they will respond in a less than favorable way. Allow the other being a chance to interact with you in a way that supplies positive energy to both parties.

Nature beings allow their interactions to be about positive influences, not negative interactions. They will not engage with you in less than productive ways. If this is the case for them or what they see in you, they will not interact with you at all or they will simply ask you to leave them alone. In later chapters, there are descriptions of situations I have encountered such as these and if those interactions occur, I simply suggest you walk away. It is always better to interact with someone who *wants* to interact with you, rather than engage in a situation that calls for force or intimidation. This advice can be applied to any energy exchange among people, animals, or plant life. In the case of nature beings, they will simply not show up when you ask them to or you will receive the negative energy they are emitting, if the negativity is coming from them. In most cases, it is our desire to want to force them to talk with us and they just simply won't. The best way to engage is to be engaging. That is solid universal wisdom for all situations.

Man did not weave the web of life – he is merely a strand in it. Whatever he does to the web, he does to himself.

- Chief Sealth

Nature beings implore respect among all beings. This is the best method of learning to relate to other entities in any realm. Respect is inherent in many cultures and nature beings are no exception. They make themselves much more available to those who show respect for who they are and what they provide to our world. Opening your mind includes offering respect and honoring other entities for their existence, no matter the shape, size or role they play. Nature beings allow for mishaps and when they see your true heart, that is enough for them to continue a dialogue in the natural realm.

Nature beings will communicate with people in several different ways. Their communication can be similar to other entities in that you may see them, you may hear them, you may smell them, you may feel them, and sometimes you just know they are there. Seeing beings in their non-physical state requires some practice and keen observation skills. This is called *clairvoyance*. Clairvoyance comes easy for some as it is their primary means of communication. These people tend to be visual learners, prefer looking at art, movies, and physical objects to understand them, and see the world clearly in their mind's eye as well as their physical eye. The mind's eye and physical eye become one and the same for many clairvoyants.

Clairaudience is the ability to hear things. Sometimes that includes hearing something outside yourself, as well as hearing words and thoughts inside your mind. Clairaudients prefer sounds of music, nature, and being read to or reading aloud rather than watching something or feeling it in their hands. Clairaudients also like to listen for thoughts instead of getting visual images to understand other beings. They hear undertones in someone's voice and pick up on auditory cues from the world around them.

Clairsentients are feelers, people who feel everything around them. They are sensitive to feeling energy, auras, and malevolent energy off other beings. Clairsentients feel energy and information when they hold an object or touch something. In a crowd, clairsentients will feel overwhelmed due to all the energy they are feeling around them. Clairsentients also get vibrations from people and objects that allow them to sense the meaning inside that object.

Claircognizants employ the ability to just know something. They don't know how they know it or why, they just do. Information will come to them in a deep sense of knowing and they won't know how that information came to them or the meaning behind it. Many times, claircognizants will feel the energy in their gut or in their heart and know how to act based upon what they already know. Claircognizants also have the ability to foretell knowledge about future events, past situations, and present meantimes in relation to the situation - as it currently presents itself. Claircognizants also know how to deal with a situation based upon past references they sometimes have no idea how they got. These situations are unique in that only claircognizance will allow someone to open to a new dimension of telling information. It can be rare to include the source of knowing, yet many claircognizants today are learning to decipher the whereabouts of their information sources.

All beings have the ability to receive information in all four ways: seeing, hearing, feeling, and knowing. Each of us has a primary means of communicating within the energy sphere and each of us can develop all four, if we choose. When you receive information and communication from nature beings, they will communicate with you in the easiest way that you will receive their communication. Verbal is not necessary as the other four categories are not only sufficient, but more accurate and more precise in deciphering the true meaning of the communication. Telepathic communication is by far the simplest and most widely used form of communication among all beings, whether it is recognized or not. We all have thoughts, feelings, knowings, and visual cues about what is happening in our personal world; it is a matter of to what extent would you like to develop these and gain new understanding from other entities besides humans. As humans, we decided long ago that vocal information would somehow suffice and allow us to interpret information better. This is not the case. How many times have you felt misunderstood or miscommunicated something to someone or had to talk yourself in or out of something? Talk is not cheap; it actually requires loads more energy than simple energetic transfers. How many times have you heard about someone who at first instance didn't trust somebody they first met because they had a "feeling" something wasn't right, but the person was able to "put their mind at ease" by talking to them? And later they found out that person wasn't trustworthy and they should have followed their first instinct. We all carry energetic patterns around us that tell everyone else exactly who we are in that moment, past, present, and future. Words can be easily manipulated, but energy patterns are pretty straightforward in most cases. Learning to decipher them can be a little more challenging the longer we have put our telepathic meters undercover. Still, it can be relearned easily with a little practice, trust and understanding.

Trust is the next step in learning to communicate with nature beings. When you receive a communication or what you believe to be a communication, don't dismiss it. Acknowledge it, thank the entity for engaging with you, and trust that what you received was the correct information for you. It always is. Sometimes, it may come across a little muddled until you fine-tune your perceptive abilities, but always know that what you received is the right message for you. And keep trying, again and again. The nature beings will practice with you, for they are learning too and time is not an issue for them. They still have their work to do, but they will come back and visit with you again. When you are first beginning to experience the different nature beings, information will come across in one of the four ways just previously mentioned, whatever is easiest for you to receive. You may hear something in the form of a word or thought. You may see a nature being and/or their energy, or see words form in your head. Some people receive visual images from the nature beings. You may just feel the presence of a nature being or feel their joy coming across to you. Sometimes, you may just know that someone is there and that they are associated with a particular event or a particular physical nature body. You will intrinsically know if they are happy or sad. Sometimes, you will receive information and messages in all four ways or in multiple ways at once. I have trained myself to receive information in all four ways, as well as others not mentioned, and you can do the same.

If you suspect you are clairvoyant, open your mind to any visual image that may come or just sit quietly and see what you see. You may see an outline around a nature body or the nature being itself, energy coming off a tree or rock, or the nature being may send you images to tell you their story. Open your mind to what you receive.

If you suspect you are claircognizant, know that what you receive is genuine information and even though you may not recognize the source, trust what you receive. Many times, claircognizants like to train themselves in other disciplines to allow them to receive clarity on their information, but this is not always true for all claircognizants. Trust what you decide for yourself and you will receive the most beautiful messages. You may walk into an area and just know what happened to create a nature preserve or know why the nature being associated with an individual tree in a meadow chose to create their life that way. Trust what you receive and know that what comes is true for you.

If you think you might be clairsentient, then feel your way through the forest. Feel the trees and leaves and dirt. When you go to the beach, feel the sand in your toes and the water on your hands. Sit and feel the energy around your body as it permeates in and out of your being. Feel, feel, feel. Clairsentients in nature are touchers and experiencers. When you touch a tree or a rock, you automatically feel their life story or you feel how powerful the energy running down the river is. You can feel the emotions and thoughts of the nature being as they communicate with you, so allow yourself to feel their experience as yours. This will allow you to receive more next time you engage with nature.

If you know you are clairaudient, then thoughts, words, voices, and music will be your primary connection to nature. When you engage with the nature beings, ask them to send you messages and thoughts, then clear your mind and hear what you hear. It is like listening on the end of a telephone. You say something and then you wait for what that person is going to say without thinking or anticipating their answer. Just hear it as it comes.

If you do or want to receive in all four ways or others, simply ask for a communication and know yourself well enough to trust whatever way it will come. When I engage with nature, I will sit next to a tree or in a field and open to what will come next. When I begin to communicate with a nature being, many times I will see the being first, and then hear words in my head. Sometimes the words come across as sounds, other times I see them written across the darkness in my mind. Sometimes they will then send me visual images of their work or their story and I will feel the energy of the area and the emotions associated with what was experienced. There are times I will walk into an area and just know that there is energy in a specific place or a nature being off to my left, or right, or wherever. It can be amazing when you learn to use all four communication methods simultaneously because your ability to receive will increase tremendously and if one method is not working or is becoming overwhelming, the other three will kick in where the others left off and fill in the gaps. It becomes a much more rich and multidimensional experience when you receive in multiple ways. It is akin to going from watching a silent movie, to watching a movie with sound, to being in the movie with sound and images, to real life where you feel and experience everything you see, hear and know to be true.

A chief event of life is the day in which we have encountered a mind that startled us.

- Ralph Waldo Emerson

Do not try to force yourself to learn all four methods, just open yourself to them and ask the Universe and your guides to help you. The nature beings will help you too. Many of them will play with you as you learn to experience life in different ways. They enjoy this as much as you do. Ask for more experiences with the nature beings and ask for them in different ways and when you've asked for more, just allow the experiences to come in whatever ways they do. Know that they will be there and be patient with yourself and your connections as you relearn new methods. The experiences you have with the nature beings will allow you to experience more and more aspects of life in a whole new way.

They want to engage with you and they want to be a part of your life. All you have to do is ask. Then trust, experience, know it to be true, and ask for more. It's that simple. I know you can do it too.

Five keys to working and communicating with nature beings:

- *Spend time in or with nature.*
- *Opening your mind, minding your thoughts.*
- *Four ways to experience non-physical beings:*
    Feel, see, hear, know.
- *Trust what you receive.*
- *Ask for more.*

AUTHOR'S NOTE

While reading this book, there may be terms that you come across that are unfamiliar or used in non-conventional ways. As I was receiving messages, there would come many times when I would open up a dictionary to decipher the meaning behind a chosen word. Rest assured that the words you read are the very words I did receive from the nature beings and they are the correct ones. Nature beings, like Angels, spirit guides and other non-physicals, choose their words very specifically because they know how limiting a word can be. If we all related to one another solely through feelings and personal expression, there would be little room for error in interpreting a message. However, that does not come across as well in written format. If a word seems out of place or unfitting, I suggest you either feel the meaning within yourself and see what answer you get, or look it up. I also suggest looking up the roots of the words used and their meanings to decipher more information. I guarantee you will find the meaning behind their messages clearly either way you go about seeking the answer to your question. Or simply go ask them yourself.

Believe nothing. No matter where you read it, or who said it, no matter if I have said it, unless it agrees with your own reason and your own common sense.

– Buddha

*Sometimes thou may'st walk in Groves, which being full
of Majestie will much advance the Soul.*

*- Thomas Vaughan,
Anima Magica Abscondita*

WATER

Water beings are exclusive to their area and genuinely protective of what they are doing and why. Most water beings are very easy to communicate with and readily want to speak with people because we are so closely and intimately connected. There are many types of water beings and water energy protectors including water sprites, fairies, animal guardians, merpeople and so many more, yet there are also water beings who prefer to oversee and maintain specific areas of water or water energy. Their job tends to be to protect, cleanse, and purify the waterways and many of them want to open a dialogue about their lives and how we can help one another.

Water beings leave areas unmarked and unscathed by their existence and they want to teach people how to do the same. Many water beings wait patiently to talk to other beings wanting to learn more about water, water supplies, and how our oceans, lakes, streams and rivers intersect and create life. The energy of water is specific in that it gives life energetically and physically, and when in motion it has great power to create, break down, and rebuild. More than just protecting our water sources, water beings live to create energy and maintain its flow. Water beings are highly abundant and anywhere there is a water source, including your home, there are lots and lots of water beings nearby working to maintain and perpetuate that water's existence.

PERSONAL MESSAGES FROM THE WATER BEINGS

Sometimes water beings, just like spirit guides and Archangels, have personal messages for us for the situations we are involved in or with guidance that we need. While preparing to write this book, I was volunteering as a beach naturalist at a local beach. I journeyed to an isolated section of the beach found only during low tide to see what sea life could be found. On my journey, I stopped and took a moment to talk with the ocean and give my thanks for such incredible beauty. As I stood quietly gazing, I noticed the water sprites dancing and up walked a water being. This water being walked with its energetic right arm straight out and walked straight up to me and placed its right hand on my chest over my heart chakra and said straight out to me, "You need to open your heart to people." I could feel energy being transferred to me from this incredible being and just as quickly as the being walked up, it walked away. I was actually a little surprised that this ocean being did not have more to say to me, but the message was very clear. At this particular time, I was struggling with opening myself up to people and speaking my own message freely. I had volunteered as a beach naturalist and yet, as much as I loved the water and the animals and all the fascinating information, I was terrified of talking to people about the new things I had learned for fear that I did not know enough. After realizing this fact, I smiled and laughed at myself a little, thanked the ocean being, and headed back to a busier section of the beach. I ended up having a very pleasant conversation with a man who had brought his daughter to the beach because she loved the sea so much. He had some questions which I answered as best I could and enjoyed the rest of my day simply because I trusted myself and the great gift the ocean being gave me that day.

Getting personal messages from the water beings can be life transforming, or it can simply be a gentle conversation between two souls. The water beings have lots of wonderful advice to give and they are willing to help if you ask them to. As with any other beings, there are those who wish to help more than others. Not all water beings will have profound advice, but if you keep yourself open to new events and great messages, more and more will come your way. There are so many beings waiting to assist you, you just need to believe you are worthy of that assistance and then ask for the help. They will come, that I promise you.

In one drop of water are found all the secrets of all the oceans.

- Kahlil Gibran

THE NATURE OF WATER BEINGS

Most water beings look remarkably like humans, in form, and rarely do they inhabit the actual body of water they are working with. Of course, there are always exceptions and I have met a few water beings who are deeply immersed in their physical existence, but most choose to work independently of their physicalness. Many times you can see them walking or floating across their water body and they look fluid and clear as the water is. They do not really take a shape, nor a gender, and what you see will be based upon your decided perception of them. Nonetheless, they do exist and they are very much real and they will come to you in whatever form you ask them to, if in form at all.

Water beings are exceptionally adept at communicating with human beings. Well before the days of Atlantis, we as a physical group have worked with and lived in, around, and through water. Many beings closely related to us, and those who have worked with us for millennia, still live in and around water, such as water animals (dolphins, whales, sharks), merpeople, and water beings. Practice talking to and receiving messages from the water beings, as they are easy to communicate with and are readily available anywhere water is, which is everywhere! Oceans, lakes, rivers, areas where it rains, puddles, and even a glass of water or your bathtub. They are there and will communicate with you if you open up to them. The transient water beings that move with puddles, raindrops, and glasses of water can be a little more difficult to communicate with as they tend to be quite free in their movement and energy and their purpose is significantly different than ocean or river beings. They still have a message for you and they will most likely wish to communicate with you, but it may be more free-flowing. Just try it and see what comes.

The more "permanent" water beings usually have a much stronger message about the work they are doing because their dedication is focused on perpetual cleansing and they want to engage you in helping to ease the burden for all beings. Ocean beings, river beings, lake beings, and stream beings are excellent for beginners. In fact, these beings will often seek you out if you spend time near their body of water and open yourself to the communication. However, you can just as easily practice in your home. If you have a fountain, you have a water being overseeing it. If you place a glass or bottle of water near your bed at night, the water being inhabiting that water will talk with you while you sleep. You can also go to a lake, river, or stream near your home and find water beings there managing that area. However, be forewarned that if you go into nature expecting to speak to only one being, good luck! In a forested place with a stream, there will be an infinite number of beings ready to talk with you including tree beings, water beings, rock beings, plant beings, flower beings, sunbeam beings, wind beings, and so on. It could be a whole chorus that comes to see you, so enjoy!

WATER SPRITES

The first water beings I ever saw were water sprites. Water sprites like to dance on top of the water in rivers, lakes and on the ocean. You can see them easily by looking closely at the sparkles on glistening water. They are always with the water, but it is easiest to see them when they are dancing on the ripples. Sometimes you will see hundreds, maybe even thousands, especially in highly charged water near vortexes or on the ocean, and sometimes there are only a few, such as those found in a glass of water, puddles, and fountains. The water sprites love to dance and play just as fairies do and they like to sing. In fact, the message they sent me came through in song:

"We love to dance. We love to play. We love to sing our song.
Hear us play with water our way to make the heavens come-along.
We sing, we dance, we play our tune, along the river so clear,
We laugh, we dance, we sing our song to hear our heavens up near.
We sing our song to those who hear and dance for all to see,
We laugh, we play, we do our day in lasting harmony."

What sweet sentiment! I could hear them sing their song as they went about dancing on the water ripples. The water sprites have beautiful white water wings, much like fairy wings or dragonfly wings and they wear a liquid gossamer gown on a free-flowing water body. Many water sprites have a distinctly feminine energy, yet as with anything, there are of course water sprites with masculine energy. Water sprites move freely about the water's edge and mostly they spend time charging the water with energy, love, and infusing it with their beautiful spirits. They love their water and other water beings and they invite you to come and play with them in their water. They will infuse you with loving water energy if you ask them to and play with you while you are in or near the water.

Water sprites also really love water animals and can be seen or felt playing with ducks, geese, fish, dolphins, whales, and many other water creatures. Listen for their song and watch for the sparkles on the ripples to begin a lasting relationship with the water sprites.

BLENDED WATER BEINGS

Special kinds of water beings are the blended water beings that inhabit areas of the world where water combines from more than one source. These beings have different kinds of messages and information than those who are specific to a single type of water. Blended water beings can include tributary beings, sound beings, bay beings, sea beings, strait beings, watershed beings who oversee entire areas of several types of water, drainage ditch beings, fresh and salt water conversion beings, and on and on and on.

There are also beings who live in the areas that contain locks and channels where boats go from one body of water to another. I met one such being on a trip to the Hiram M. Chittendam Locks in Seattle. The locks allow boats to flow from fresh water Lake Union to salt water Puget Sound and back. There are salmon that also use this waterway going to the ocean to grow and coming back to their rivers to spawn. I could see this water being moving in and out of the actual locks and took a moment to connect with him while he was working. He told me his job was to measure the activity and to protect, guide, and guard the channel itself. He told me he had a slightly different purpose than other water beings because there is significance and importance to keeping the locks in motion. His purpose is to help us by protecting our water transfers, food supplies (with the fish and deliveries), and maintain an equal balance of energy proportion in the area. He told me that his primary duty was to maintain the balance of the human needs for the water in that area with the needs of the water itself. When my water friend and I sat down to have a conversation, this is what he had to say:

"The water itself is cleansed and purified by other beings. My job is to promote and protect what exists as it moves quickly and freely from one source to another. We, as water beings, work to maintain balance, but my job is about balancing human life and human needs with the needs of the water. This type of work is done all along coastlines of America, yet channel beings move energy more

rapidly and we expect to do it solely. Few humans offer help in this arena and we do not expect change. We do not need the help as other water bodies do. The energy moves through here quickly and ferociously. We can adapt to what needs to be balanced much more quickly than asking for assistance. It all changes so quickly on both sides of the water/human needs. Balance is easily attainable. That is why you see only one of me. Many other bodies of water have greater need. This area is quite clean and diverse in energy terms. I must work now. Thank you for talking to me. Come back soon."

I told my friend goodbye and back to work he went. I was glad he answered the question I had thought earlier about why I only saw one water being in the area. There were water sprites down below and lake beings working on Lake Union, but in the actual locks, I could only see one being, which I thought to be unusual. His message clarified what I was thinking and opened me up to yet another aspect of the wonderful world of water beings.

A SPECIAL SIDENOTE ABOUT USING WATER

As funny as it seems, I have been asked, "What happens to the water beings when we drink the water out of the glass?" At first I thought this to be a funny question, but then I started to wonder that myself. Once, I had talked with a puddle being after a brief rainstorm. I thought about how the puddle was small and when the sun came out, it would evaporate and return to the air. The puddle being showed me that the water beings that are transient just move from water to water, or energy place to energy place. They are not forced to stay with a specific body of water or watch it pass through our body as we absorb the glass of water. I was told that once we absorb the water into our system, or simply by the act of drinking it, we become the guardians of that energy (the water) until it leaves our body and the water beings leave and find other sources of water or return to Source until they are ready to move on to a new project. Some water beings will work with the air beings to guide the energy as it evaporates into steam and moves back to the atmosphere, others will just move on. It is not required that there has to be beings watching over and guiding physical and non-physical energy, however it makes the process smoother and more efficient when there is someone or something standing by to love it, lift it, and encourage it onward.

I am in love with the green earth.

– Charles Lamb

EARTH

Earth beings are in and of the earth itself. Earth beings sing to the earth and create harmonic convergences wherever possible to allow greater energy to flow in and out of the earth's energy fields. Earth beings come in a multitude of varieties including earth messengers, earth healers, earth workers/demonstrators, and energetic earth beings. Of course, there are a great many more, but these are the four that will be discussed in this chapter.

There is no need for temples, no need for complicated philosophies. My brain and my heart are my temples; my philosophy is kindness.

- Dalai Lama

EARTH MESSENGERS

Earth messengers work to promote harmony and create allowances for Divine messages to enter into cognition among earth dwellers. Earth messengers live within the earth and provide harmony and understanding among all beings who work within earth's core energy fields. The earth itself has consciousness and resolution, so the earth messengers work tirelessly to promote and provide sustenance in the form of energy healing to the earth. This type of energy healing is promoted through earth humans to provide energy transformation and energy likeness akin to earth energy. Earth energy is precious in that it is unique in its form. There is no other energy like earth energy anywhere else in the planetary alignments and earth messengers provide constitutions that allow the earth to continue providing this energy. Earth messengers know there are no limits to earth energy and they provide information to earth humans that want to bring more energy awareness to it. These messengers, of earth origin and human alike, provide unlimited resources to all mankind in terms of service, gratitude, graciousness, and kindness. These types of energy allow the earth to continue fulfilling her own "destiny" in terms of energy output and collection.

Earth messengers bring unique, individual messages to humans through means of inspired ideas, inspirational thoughts, wired communications, and rough translations of older ideals. These ideas, thoughts, and communications involve the earth and earth matters in terms of energy welfare, energy harnessing, and energy manipulations. We, as earthly human messengers, provide the avenue for those messages to be vocalized into patterns of change. Earth messengers are few, although there are many human earth messengers available to provide the insights they receive from those in non-physical.

The first time I met the team of earth messengers, I was with a friend in Sedona and we were sitting below Bell Rock enjoying the view and the energy of the vortex there. My friend and I decided to meditate and just experience whatever came during the meditation. As I closed my eyes, I could feel the energy of the earth pulling me down into the core and when I arrived there, I could see a team of beings working hard to put out messages and ideas and communications to the world at-large. They were very busy and engaged in their activity, so I just observed and watched them working. Finally, one being approached me and I asked what kind of beings they were and I was told they were earth messengers. This was quite a new concept for me, but at this point, not much surprised me anymore, as there was too much awe in the universe to waste time with shock.

I sat with the earth messengers for a short time and almost as abruptly as I came into their existence, I was thrust back out into the area around Bell Rock. When my friend arose out of her meditation, I told her what I saw. I explained that the earth messengers I saw looked much like an outline of human energy/form and water beings, although they had much more intensity, although light-heartedness, to their energy. It was like sitting in a room of people brainstorming and sending out ideas into the room, almost like a cosmic mailroom. There were thoughts in transition, thoughts being processed, ideas being formed and messages coming to them from other sources. It was an amazing spectacle of planetary and universal exchange happening. These beings were definitely unlike any other non-physical I had encountered so far. It was a fantastic experience and a fabulous invitation into the greater workings of earth.

Since I had not received a message from the earth messengers other than an observation of their activities, I knew at some point I wanted to spend time with them again. After I returned home and began writing and spending time with other nature beings, I wondered when I would get the opportunity to engage with them again. I did not have the sense that I would seek them out, but that they would come to visit me one day.

One morning, three months after my first encounter, I had turned on my computer to begin writing and I knew I wanted to work on this chapter and write about my experiences with the earth beings. I began writing and no matter what I did, I could not sit still. I felt as though I had downed a truckload of caffeinated beverages and topped it off with a few barrels of sugar. My energy was just surging. I couldn't sit still and I was having trouble writing and being clear, so I decided to putter around the house and then take a shower. The energy was climbing higher and higher and I was beginning to get a little concerned for my own welfare, as I had no idea what was going on. After my shower, I knew all I wanted to do was write, so I sat down and began typing. I began writing the first few paragraphs and all of a sudden, in the middle of a sentence, I began to receive a message and I knew it was from an earth messenger. The energy was so strong and so determined, I had to stop a few times to take deep breaths and regain my own composure. As I was receiving the message, I looked around to see the nature being it was coming from and because the energy surge was so strong and so intent, I could not see the being, all I could do was write.

This is what the earth messenger had to say:

"Earth translators, as many non-physicals call us, provide messages from the non-physicals we hear or encounter. We provide messages of relief, resignation to better ideas, and counteractions to better earthly ideals about how to raise this planet's vibration as a whole. We provide security and insight into many earthly matters from technology to vehicular choices to random choices among all agreeing upon a new way for something greater. We work in harmony with those around us, physical and non-physical, earthly and non-earthly, to provide a better resource into energy manufacturing. Not manufacturing in terms of what you, as humans, call it, but manufacturing in terms of creating and building, maintaining and de-creating to make something new. We provide a lot of information about your technology we receive from other sources and we provide more insights to humans about earth construction, how the planet works, why it works and what it wants. Earth messengers are highly advanced in that they know what to do to make this world more livable and suitable for all entities. No one works with us directly, or at least it is rare. I

provide information in terms known to be thoughts, ideas, movements, and sometimes I get involved by creating hands-on, figuratively speaking. We, as messengers, provide keen insight throughout your world and we do so regularly based upon what the earth wants. She is our goddess, our sayer, our dictater, the one who dictates to us what needs to be done on earth. She provides our clarity and our insight and we pass it to you. Earth messengers are few and far between because we just provide the messages from earth to those willing to hear, those who want to hear, and those who will do something with that which they hear. There are far more earth healers and earth demonstrators than messengers, as per necessity. This is what we do. This is our purpose. We are of the earth."

After I finished the message, I could feel the energy still surging through me, yet it had been taken down about fifteen notches to a much more manageable level. I realized after finishing the message and taking a few more deep breaths, this was a short glimpse into the world of energy messengers and this is how they communicate with us. For those who are really receptive and engaged to connect with them, the energy comes through as a highly dramatic surge. My guides told me later that this is what true inspiration feels like. You just can't *not* connect with it; the energy consumes you in such a positive way. This is the work the earth messengers do. They inspire us to be more connected to ourselves, to one another, and to the earth.

For those who are still learning to be more receptive to "outside" communications, the inspiration or idea may hit them in a less dramatic fashion, yet the message is equally important. If you get a tingling or a sensation that there is something that needs your attention in regards to the earth or an idea bursts out of nowhere and you feel highly connected to it and that it is important in some way, *pay attention to it*. You have just received a communication from a non-physical entity and you can always ask the non-physical to clarify who they are, if that is important for you to know. It could be your spirit guide, an Angel, or an earth messenger. Truth is, it doesn't matter where the inspiration comes from; what matters is what you do with it.

I go to nature to be soothed and healed, and to have my senses put in order.

- John Burroughs

EARTH HEALERS

Earth healers are designated to areas of the earth that need cleansing, uplifting energy, and pressure release from blocked energetic uprisings. Energy healers are non-physical earth entities that produce energy flow and construction along a myriad of lines in the earth's core, surface, and other regions. Energy flow produces destruction of old energy patterns, as well as creates new lines of uplifting, upbeat energy waves that cross the globe. Energy healers work to produce more of these lines and waves of energy patterns across the sphere. Energy healers look like other earth entities in that they are dark in aura color, exuding greens, blues, and gold, and they produce unlimited amounts of energy through their beingness to connect to the "outer" world. Energy beings have a high source of potential energy awaiting their every wish and choose where that energy needs to be placed across the lines. Energy patterns move and flow easily around the atmosphere and penetrate the earth to the core with force and grace. It's a beautiful combination of soulless energy arriving at its destination. It is the perfect exaltation of abundant grace and energetic balance in all that is. Energy healers are critical for our continuation and they should be considered whenever energy needs to be replaced or manifested in an area of the earth that is diminished or in need of resupply.

Energy healers can be accessed easily and frequently for personal needs too. They can provide a home with energy increases and they can provide personal energy uplifts. Mostly they work with earth energy, but earth energy is highly healing to earth entities. Many of us call upon Angelic entities to replenish our supply of needed energy and clear away old energetic debris, however earth energy healers can and will supply necessary energy to those who ask. They allow you to consume and reuse Mother

Earth energy and sustain yourself with earth's healing properties. Call upon them for cleansing, clearing, and purifying your thoughts, imbalances, imperfections, and anything you wish to clear away. They will uplift and inspire you to become one with them.

"Energy healing is one of the oldest forms of healing arts in existence across many planes. Energy healers on earth do much of the same work in alchemical ways to allow earth entities to thrive and become alive in all that they do and all they provide. Earth energies are charismatic and prospiring in ways yet seen. Earth energy is for all to use and much like other beings, we resupply necessary energy to the earth and all its inhabitants. We allow energy to resimulate and recalcitrate upon its surfaces and allow new energy forms to emerge. We engage with those who call upon us although many do in other forms. We are called by many other names; this is our origin, of the earth. We allow others to call for our needs and we recant those needs to those who ask for our assistance. We engage with many types of entities across all lines and places. We explore new avenues of energy transfers and healings. Healing is not considered what you assume it to mean on your planet. We call healing, of the earth's field. It is a oneness and an exaltation of energy in its purest form. Healing is not about curing or disarming. Healing is about purity and purifying one's truth. Healing is about oneness and truthful expression in ways that we provide with the earth's energy. We clean, we purify, we

heal, we exist. This is our purpose and we engage you to call upon us for your own healing. We shall provide that which you ask as you ask it. This is our mission to serve you, as in serving others, we serve us. Us as all. We are all. This is who we are. We are here to help you. Call upon us any time, in any place, as we are always present to be there. This is our message for you. Come to us, we shall be there."

When I was working with the energy healers, it was almost as if they were only subtly there, as they gently came in while I was writing their description. The energy healers are present everywhere and they are excited about working with us one-on-one. Energy healers are a great way to reconnect with the earth itself, but also to ourselves, as we are truly only one creation. Energy healers want to work with us and just as any other entity of healing order, we must ask for their help and assistance. They are there and available, but they will never inflict themselves upon us. That is intrusion and not how they operate. They want to inspire and interweave fabulous energy patterns within us, yet we must call to them for that experience. That's all it takes. Asking. Simple, isn't it?

♦ ♦ 🏵 ♦ ♦

When we contemplate the whole globe as one great
dewdrop, striped and dotted with continents and islands,
flying through space with other stars all singing and
shining together as one, the whole universe appears as an
infinite storm of beauty.

- John Muir (1838 - 1914)

EARTH WORKERS

Energy manifesters, energy demonstrators, and energy orators are all types of earth workers. Earth workers provide insight into how to manually change the earth's energy with respect to ours. These are the alchemists, the wizards of the nature world, the warlocks of energy matters. These energy gurus have learned to manipulate and maneuver energy in the best possible way. These are earthly helpers and they have answers to our most pressing questions about how the earth can do what it does and how we do what we do. They have special knowledge and insight into our world as it really exists that we are just beginning to understand in terms of scientific research and logical analysis. These teams of energy mavens allow our abilities to flow between one another and create energy concordances with other entities. Earth workers work to provide us with unlimited potential to manifest our greatest desires. These beings create earthly treasures, earthly workings, and earthly truths. They are truly fantastical beings who seek to work with those who want to understand energy fluctuations and energy creations. These beings can be called upon by those who wish to understand, but they will only work with you if you are ready to engage in that full understanding. There are different levels they are willing to engage in and they will work with almost anyone; it is just a matter of truth and honesty in who you are and how honest you are with yourself. These beings understand great depths of our planetary existence and they are eager to share, but you must be able to understand it before they will be willing to truly engage with you.

Many times they will show you glimpses first and see your reaction or proaction towards what they have shown you. Then based upon that information they will decide how much more you can take before it becomes too much to understand. It is a process, but one that is highly worthwhile in understanding as your life progresses to the point where you may seek more understanding. If this is your wish, then engage in enticing them to play with you. Signs will begin to show themselves first and then eventually the earth workers will find you and show you more. Study them and study the planet's true nature and this will show you the path to the earth workers.

Earth workers prefer the term "earth worker" because it is simple. There is no grandiosity to it and there is no preclusion about who they are or what they can do. They are simply what they are and this is just part of the earth's existence. Their simplicity is something we can all learn from in that they use their energy and their abilities to prevent misunderstandings and misalignments of their true nature. They are simple in their name, but make no mistake that these beings are anything but simple in their work. They have great understanding and great sympathy for our distress and our lack of remembrance of our own abilities. They would like to work with us to rekindle that, as we are ready. This is a major part of their undertaking and why they do what they do. There was a time when they had less of this to do and more time simply to play, but now they want to awaken anyone who chooses that pathway and they will walk with us in spirit along the path.

"Energy transformation is not just a game, it is the rules. These beings of light, these catchers of darkness, play to play in any way they can. We wish to bring a new breed of truth to you, for this breed is not new, it is old, very old. It is the truth that has always been and always will be. We are seekers of understanding and creation. We love to manipulate and manifest new thoughts, new ideas, new convergences. This is our playtime. This should be your playtime. You do not engage with earth energy as we do. You once did. Now you have lost that passion. Earth energy is easy to play with and manipulate in relation to the other energies of other planets. This energy is easy, mostly because it is not used. Earth uses her own energy, but the inhabitants do not. Some do. Not many. We as earth workers prefer to play most of our existence

and engage with those who seek to know what we know and those who can teach us more. We are learning also. Always learning and recounting old ways into new. We seek you because you seek us. You asked for us many, many times and you wanted to know about telekinesis, teleportation, tele-vision, telepathic guidings. This we do all times, and we wish it for you too. You are not fully ready to accept our knowledge but we show you in bits and pieces what can be done. When you are no longer surprised and it becomes second-nature, then it will be a natural progression for you. Engage in what you know now, more is coming to you. Do not be impatient; there is plenty of room for learning and knowledge in your existence. These things will come back to you when you seek greater understanding. Understand and play with what you have now and when more is available for you, we shall provide new insight. Next will be truth-telling. This energy provides much clarity into the world itself. As there is energy in thought and word, there is great power in truth telling itself. This is power manipulation. Manipulation is not what mankind has come to call it. Manipulation is about harvesting the energy for something new. Out of the old comes something new. This is manipulation. Manipulation on earth has become about negativity and deviance; this is not true in our world. Manipulation is about creation, not destruction. Call it what you wish, the same is true for either. We wish to engage with you daily if you wish it. Ask for our assistance in engaging with energy in new ways and we will provide you with insight into what to do or say next. This is our way. We will show you when you are ready. And the time is near for more information boosts. Be patient and kind with yourself. It is all about learning. You could not possibly know it all as it is always changing. Always. Progress with it and it shall progress in you. That is our key for your understanding and your next step. We shall work with you daily on this key and next you will find more. Ask us to understand that which you do not and we shall explain. It can be very simple."

As I sat with this profound and insightful message, I could feel my third eye opening larger and the energy swirling around and around in my body. The earth workers asked me to understand how to progress with it and let it progress within me. This thought alone provoked a deep shattering energy wave inside my body and inside my being that put me in a state of clarity and serenity. I thanked the earth workers for providing me with such an amazing message and promised to work with them more often. Having never met an earth worker before on an individual basis, this was a monumental experience for me. I could feel my heart chakra opening wider than it had ever opened, almost with a minute degree of discomfort and a peace in my soul that had been retreating for some time. I felt cherished, cared for, and deeply, deeply loved. The energy was so similar to the deep workings of an Archangel, but in a completely different way. The experience was most intriguing and left me to wonder what more I get to learn, what is next for me.

◆ ◆ ✦ ◆ ◆

You cannot feel yourself out of doors; plain, sky, and mountains ray beauty which you feel. You bathe in these spirit-beams, turning round and round... Presently you lose consciousness of your own separate existence: you blend with the landscape, and become part and parcel of nature.

- John Muir

I have learned much about earth beings in that they are so similar to us, yet they see so much more of the earth than we do. We have become narrow-visioned when we look at the earth and we see physical aspects, but we miss the deep intrinsic capabilities of the earth and all of its inhabitants, not just those thrust into a physical body. Earth beings provide us with a greater sense of who we are and where we have come from, not just in terms of 'the other side' or our spiritual counterparts. Our intrinsic value lies all around us in the form of nature, nature's energy, and the earth's true majesty because that is who we are too. This is a valuable lesson to be learned as most of us are trying desperately to get out of the earth and away from the chaos and misunderstandings of the energy here. That would no longer be the case if we really see and experience what the earth has to offer. It is more than just a place of beauty and sustenance. It provides us energetically with life-giving essence, and the nature beings who claim the earth as their home and of their creating have much to teach us about really living.

To be free is important, but to help others be free is more important.

- Elie Wiesel

ENERGETIC EARTH BEINGS

Energetic earth beings are similar to other earth beings in that they provide energy resources, energy uplifts, and energy relocations, yet they also provide energy manufacturing that other earth beings do not create. Energetic earth beings use their energy to promote source information and download prior thoughts from one position to another. They move thoughts, ideas, and emotions from location to location within their global resource spheres. They are predominantly trained to perform kindness acts upon those who wish their assistance, although they are capable of alternative means of destruction should they be called upon for that as well. Energetic earth beings provide resource information through likened mannerisms that accentuate nervous (static) energy into positive (free-flowing) energy. This energy can come from the earth itself or from its inhabitants such as people, animals, and plants. Nervous energy is not simply for physical entities; it is an energy that is felt throughout the globe in various fashions, including and especially among earth beings. Earth beings feel their experiences as they experience them, much like humans, although they are readily more available to dissociate from their actual experience, unlike humans prefer or choose to do. Energetic earth beings relate and consume unwanted desires into magical properties. They are closely tied to mystical sea beings and earth workers as they provide their unique services.

You will find that energetic earth beings are similar to energy beings, as they are related, yet they are not the same. Energetic earth beings provide resource and energy relocation to and from the earth itself. Energy beings have a much more expansive role and broader abilities within the universal scheme. You can call upon either for energy manipulation and desires, yet energetic earth beings will aid you first, simply because we are all working so closely together for the earth.

Energetic earth beings are similar in color and appearance to other earth beings, yet they differ dramatically in how they process their work. They are consumers and doers. They take their work seriously because it tends to be more delicate in its nature. Energetic earth beings are not all alike, yet they have similar missions: to change and upheave energy into its opposite emotion, thought, and form. They take negative emotions, negative thoughts, negative outcomes and introduce positive inquiries and positive lightness into a being, so it can become stronger, more adept, more resolute about its own mission. Not all energetic earth beings do this particular type of work, as there are other energetic earth beings who focus on alternative outcomes of energy consumption. They can just as easily take positive, uplifting energy and use it to destroy, which is just an alternate form of creating. For the purpose of this book and the work inscribed herein, I have chosen to work with the energetic earth beings who create positive outcomes from negative energy and these are the ones we shall discuss.

Once again, as I was writing their description, the earth beings came fully through before I was finished writing and ready to receive. There is something special about the energy and presence of earth beings. They are subtle and shy in their demeanor, yet their messages are strikingly profound and unequivocally unique. The energetic earth beings moved in and out of my consciousness as I finished my thoughts and sentences and this is the message they so patiently waited to give me:

"We, the energy beings of light, we are the bearers of soul transformation. We change those who wish and seek our assistance in ways that can be considered miraculous if given and received inside ourselves. We beings of giving light and energy provide much resource assistance to those who request our help. We provide insight, condition acquaintance, and resource allocation

to all when requested, but it must be asked for. Our energy is for all and those who seek it will learn to use it as we have and as we will teach them. This energy is profound in its entirety because it is much more than Source. It is Creation itself. It is the energy of all creation, the energy of magnitude, the energy of right thinking. We are proud in our creation as our creators are proud in it. This energy is not for the meek or the mild to consume; it must be taken in quickly and used bountilessly. This energy can transform and change even that which is thought to no longer be movable. It is magnanimous. When we seek to reassure someone of their beingness, this energy comes out in its entirety. It comes out pure and strong and with one false pretense: to shine. Shining is not for the weak and mild. Shining is for those who seek power and security. Shining is done with grace and wisdom, if the seeker can handle its power. There is much grace in handling the bigger energies before they overcome you. We seek to give power to those who wish to use it for benevolent means. This energy can be used in many, many ways, yet we are benevolent beings. This energy will transform and reassure you of your own power if used properly. Allow us to grace you with our gift and we will show you many things in your world that you have not seen. Allow us to enter into your home and abode and clean out impurities of energy and light that do not transform you for greater good and higher power. Our power will cleanse and celebrate your entirety as you truly exist in this plane. This is our gift to you. Ask and call upon us any who wish for enlightenment, truth, and severity in their *transformation. This is what we do, to and for you. This is our power."*

Their message spoke of grace and power and they with equal magnitude in their presence. These beings of energy and light, as they call it, are powerful, powerful entities who seek to share their knowledge and wisdom with those who wish greater truths, greater understandings, and higher wisdom. They do not wish to give power in a place where it cannot be handled or used benevolently, yet they will give it as it is asked for. When they spoke of shining as its one downfall, the energetic earth beings spoke of profound power and that in learning to shine, one must use wisdom and grace or it can consume you into nothingness. And that nothingness is no longer you, the you you are striving to become. These beings seek to enlighten us with our own earth energy, energy that we all share, yet few of us have truly turned on. This energy can be magnified in any number of ways once it is turned on and we can do with it what and how we choose. That is what free will is. Yet when we become consumed by it, it changes us and our motives. It becomes a means to an end instead of a journey along the path to the right end.

When we try to pick out anything by itself,
we find it hitched to everything else in the universe.

- John Muir

When the earth beings began their recent continuous communication with human beings, it was received with little to no reception. The earth beings have long asked for our assistance, as we are all inhabitants of the same planetary existence. They offer themselves to us to assist us on our own journey and in return they ask for promises to prepare and supply the earth with loving kindness and great achievement. As a path to right-heartedness, our complimentary attitude toward their work will allow both types of entities to work in harmony with one another and as one. Each layer exists to promote itself into a greater being and thus, taking moments to hear them and explore their world, as it is ours, we focus on becoming unified, whole, and magnified throughout all existence. Earth beings seek our attention only as we prepare ours for adaptation to them and their creations. By working in harmony with all existence, we will find ourselves in greater harmony with ourselves and all that is one. This will be our greatest reward for pretending to be nothing more than our true selves.

Climb the mountains and get their good tidings. Nature's peace will flow into you as sunshine flows into trees. The winds will blow their own freshness into you and the storms their energy, while cares will drop off like autumn leaves.

- John Muir

WIND AND AIR

Wind beings look like the wind. They are airy, light-filled beings with quick movements and depending on what they are doing, some are very easygoing, as a breeze, and some are much more passionate and dedicated, like windstorms. Wind beings have a purpose of change and freeing the earth of energetic and physical pollution and movement of airborne particles. They create movement in a fast-paced, dynamic way and move quickly around the earth to bring change and carry new life. They grasp the relativity of this earth plane from a physically higher perspective, as well as a more open dynamic. They have specific messages of moving and growing through change and grace as though they are inevitable, although they are fully aware of free will and individual choice. Inevitability is used more as term of what is to come by allowing greater things to happen in our physical domain.

You can experience the wind beings anytime, anywhere there is air moving, which of course is everywhere! Practice by first feeling them, then ask for movement changes in the wind around you. Wind beings love to play with people and provide freshness to, and from, our perspective. Wind beings see people as a challenge to overcome in that our energy tends to stagnate and deplete. Human beings allow themselves to deteriorate rapidly when engaged with others. Wind beings thrive on this and allow their energy to enliven all around them based upon with whom they interact. It is about teaching others to become empowered and live freely, as the air beings do.

In May of 2007, a friend and I journeyed to the Grand Canyon to enjoy the vistas and introduce my friend to the beauty and wonder of the Grand Canyon, as it was her first trip. We drove around and stopped at several viewpoints to admire and experience the energy and grandeur of the canyon and watched the sun set over the North Rim. The view was spectacular. The next morning we meandered along the South Rim, but as the day wore on a storm began to form. The wind was blowing and rain fell on and off. Several times we had to ask the wind and rain beings to allow us a few brief moments of uninterrupted viewing as we were going to leave the Grand Canyon that evening. Graciously each time, the wind and rain beings would calm the weather by ceasing to blow and pour on us, mostly for brief periods of time between a few minutes up to almost an hour. There was much activity going on that day and once during a particular windy moment, I asked for two minutes of calm weather to take in a particularly beautiful viewpoint and the wind beings agreed, but were very clear that they had work to do that day and must continue on. We honored this by accepting the brief moments given us with gratitude and not demanding more. They have their purpose and their work on this earth as much as any of us do.

The wind beings continued to give us kind gestures as we honored them and watched them work. They were very busy that day and when I asked if they had a message to pass on, this is what they had to say:

"Moving and clearing is our work today. We have much to do as there is a storm following the path we set before. We work in conjunction with many storm beings to bring about disruption equaling change and graceful movement, no matter the extreme. We work for change today. There is much to be cleared here and removed from this place of beauty. We work endlessly to preserve the natural energy of this area for this is the job we have chosen. It is our work. We work in harmony with many beings of nature to create lasting peace in this great place. It will last for more to come. We have work to do today as we clear and remove energetic debris along this crater's edge. The storm following will finish our work for this time and then we will begin again. Our message to you is clean yourselves energetically in this place or others like it to allow greater healing on this earth through your cleansings. Peace together will bring about mutual harmony among all beings as we are working towards unification of all beingness. Clean and clear your energy in places of great harmony and earth energy. There are many and they cannot be depleted for this is what we do. Seek them and seek peace in your beingness. Do not call upon us as our work is set already. You have the ability to clear all that you need within yourselves and through great places of cleansing. Go there. Those are your sources. We have our work. Go do yours. Now, we must work again."

And with that insightful message, the wind beings set themselves back into motion cleaning and clearing with such might, my friend and I had to return to the car because the wind began to blow so hard it almost blew us over. Their work may be mighty, or it may be meeker, yet the wind beings of earth have a strong desire to fulfill their purpose and maintain an equalizing harmony on our planet. This work can be done in mild, easygoing conditions or sometimes it calls for greater, awe-inspiring momentum.

All I want is to stand in a field and to smell green,
to taste air, to feel the earth want me...
- Phillip Pulfrey

On another windy occasion, I was sitting in my backyard admiring the beautiful blue summer sky and enjoying the windy breeze as it blew across my deck. I could feel the wind was quite different this time and I knew the message would have a very different tone, as this wind being was more playful and less intense about her task at hand. I watched the wind being doing her work, changing and moving the air in graceful form. This wind being was quite fully present in her wind body and enjoying every moment of it. She blew air in graceful movements and whipped it in and around trees gently and with ease. This wind being was ever so friendly and I asked her if she had anything she would like to share:

"Wind whipping in and out of trees eases life in all aspects based on movement and clarity of form. It is an art to create the wind as I do and allow free flowing movement without stagnation or interruption. Wind artists create harmony and peaceful gestures with oxygen and nitrogen and other molecules to bring life to all things. Wind artists also create joy in a breeze on a hot summer's day and coolness in the fall with the crisp breeze of autumn. Each place is different and I have seen so many. I like this area because the air changes so rapidly and with greater ease. I have less work to do!"

The wind being laughed heartily and with great joy in her work. She expressed great poetic movements and free flowing gestures about movement, change, and ease. The beauty in this wind being was she just enjoyed being. Her message was simple: joy. She spoke more like a friend than a being with a grand agenda and this may have been the greatest message of all – to just simply enjoy what you are doing while you are doing it.

Love is the ability and willingness to allow those that you care for to be what they choose for themselves without any insistence that they satisfy you.

- Wayne Dyer

The prophetic nature of wind beings lies in their very nature. They are here for change, movement, ease and grace in all that they do. Some do it with great power; others do it with gentle force, an energetic nudging. Either way, there is room to learn and work with the wind beings beyond physical conditions and physical comfort. Wind beings demonstrate how to honor yourself and your choices by moving with them in ease and grace. And when you are done with one choice, choose another; then perform that with ease and grace, as well. There is much to be learned from the many wind beings all around you. Work with them and they will bring you clarity and insight from a truly higher perspective.

We should be taught not to wait for inspiration to start a thing. Action always generates inspiration. Inspiration seldom generates action.

- Frank Tibolt

RAIN

Rain beings love to be with people, plants and animals because part of their very purpose is to provide us with liquid nourishment. The rain that falls feeds the land, which then feeds the plants, and in turn feeds the animals and people. Rain beings are plenty and come easily to anyone seeking their companionship or advice. They love to talk to people and they have a very free, fluid movement to their being, much like that of other water beings. One of the first rain beings I met came to visit me around my home in Seattle. Yes, it does rain in Seattle, yet not characteristically as much as most Seattleites would lead outsiders to believe! On one particular gray and rainy day, this rain being came to visit me while I lay looking up through my windows at the rain, the trees, and the clouds pouring down. This water being had a much lighter, freer spirit than other water beings and held his energetic hands up to the sky feeling and enjoying the rain falling down through them, much as we do when it rains. This is what he had to say:

"Blessed be the rain spirits as they fall down from the heavens to nourish your earth and our land. Blessed be the ones who receive the rain and allow it to nourish their beings and from whence they came. To those who receive it and bless it and allow it to move through them as water does in its infinite nature, they shall receive

the kindness and gentle spirit of the water and become one with those who seek Oneness. Water, especially rainwater, allows beings from many different places to feel one another more intimately. There is a connection between the water sources, and the Source that is all, when it rains because the earth, the plants, the animals, the humans, the non-physicals, the physicals, and more come together to cleanse and be free. Feel the rain as it pours heaven into your body and onto your earth. On days when it rains, more of this will be clearer to you. Pray easily on these days and stay close to your Source as you connect with one another and amongst you all (all beings). Play in the rain, it will cleanse you. Rain is for cleansing and nourishing and joy. Even acid rain returns to the earth for purity and cleansing. Trust in Source to know what to do with the impurities and yes, you will play a part in making things new. Play, play, play. There is nothing more in this life than to do just that. Play and then play some more."

The rain being began to twirl with its arms joyfully receiving the rain as it fell through them into the earth below. This beautiful spirit embodied true freedom in its soul and gave me a very profound message of love and hope and renewal for all of us, as well as a sense of peace and belonging to Source through our beautiful water supply.

May the road rise up to meet you,
may the wind always be at your back.
May the sun shine warm upon your face,
the rains fall soft upon your fields.

- Irish Blessing

Rain is something that falls almost everywhere in the world. Over oceans, over land, in the air – it's everywhere. Oceans need the water to replenish its own sources and land needs the water to renew the plants, the minerals, the toxins and other things that need to be filtered down into the earth's layers for cleansing. The cleansing that rain accomplishes for humans and other physicals isn't all that much different.

When the rain falls, it falls and produces negative ions that fill our atmosphere. These negative ions give us a sense of well-being, lightening, relaxation and calm. If you want to know more about the science of negative and positive ions, there are far better books and writers who relish the subject and can fill you with your desired knowledge. However, in this book, my desire for you to know about these negative ions that fill the air when rain begins to fall is that it is something that is uniquely important to our health and our well-being. Rain puts it this way:

"To cherish your well-being is of utmost importance and our role in your beingness is equally important to your role in ours. Your bodies fill with these ions and atoms and various chemicals and molecules to make your body feel at its best. However, with our assistance, we can grace your beingness – not your body – with a light-filled air of importance and gracefulness that even your body does not know exists. We fill you with hopeful attitudes, a wistful nature for living and everything in between. We do not lead you to believe that by being in the rain will your life become perfection. Instead, we lead you to believe that perfection lies within the rain as much as it already lies within you and our being together allows our perfection to radiate in ions."

These negative and positive ions that fill our lives, just as negative and positive emotions and situations fill our lives as well, bring us the knowledge that our happiness is not so much dictated by our situations, but by the advantage we make and take within those situations. We can choose to walk barefoot in the rain. We can choose a life filled with chaos and derision. We can choose to see the world for what it really is and has always been. We can choose to stay separate and unengaged. Either way, the choice is fully ours. And the life we will live will be the one we alone create.

I believe that there is a subtle magnetism in Nature,

which, if we unconsciously yield to it,

will direct us aright.

- Henry David Thoreau

RIVERS

Another type of water being who loves to talk to people are those who keep a watchful eye on bodies of moving water, such as rivers, creeks, and streams. One water being I met on a recent trip with a friend to Sedona inhabited a specific area of well-known Oak Creek. As I sat watching the water flow by, I felt a presence walking up the river. I greeted the water being and he came to sit with me on the rock I was on. This particular water being had very strong masculine energy, but each being, as with all beings, can have feminine energy, masculine energy, a combination of both or switch back and forth based on need or desire. The Oak Creek water being was very friendly and receptive to communicating with me and he told me he had a message for both me and my friend. The water being's message was about cleaning our home water supply and that the filters we had currently were not pure enough. The water being continued by expressing that we needed to "clean our homes" with our water and that included our physical homes as well as our bodies, and this could be done by purifying our water supply "just as the water runs clean and is filtered through the river." The water being thanked us for our concern and understanding of water and he told me that he lived in this particular stretch of Oak Creek and that he loved talking with people. In this area of Oak Creek, my friend and I both had multiple visits from fairies, bats, and dragonflies, all guardians of the water. This was the Oak Creek water being's message:

"Yes, you are welcome here. This is sacred ground for us water beings as this area is greatly connected to Mother Earth. Mother Earth speaks with us/through us often. She seeks healing of her planet, as we seek cleaning of our waters. You can clean by filtering, you can clean by washing, you can clean by using your bodies with energy. We just ask that you do so with love and honor the water as it comes from Source. Regular filters are not strong enough, but they are close. More filters are not the answer; better filters are better for your bodies. The answer lies in cleaning the waters. This can be done through healings and honorings and watching over the precious supply. The supply is infinite, but a safe supply can be limited unless it is properly cleansed. Run the water through your hands and let it pour through you. Feel it. Taste it. Know that it is the same energy as you are. And purify it with your love. This will honor the water. Do this as a way of making the act of taking water sacred. Be fastidious in your care for water. Cleaning your water will clean your bodies will clean your energy and cleaning your energy will clean your bodies will clean your water. It is cyclic and deeply interconnected. Honor your water. Honor our water."

This water being, as many water beings and water animals do, possessed a great amount of love and peace in regard to us and the earth. There is a great continual request for more peace on our planet and the water beings are deeply involved in creating that change.

Eventually, all things merge into one,
and a river runs through it.

- Norman Maclean

Water beings are not the same everywhere you go. They have different ideas, different thoughts, different jobs. They want to express themselves just as we do – in their own unique way.

On a recent trip to Denver, my mom and I took a little side trip to the mountains and went for an afternoon drive. We just wanted to see what we'd see and come across whatever entities, human or otherwise, that we might encounter. We didn't have an agenda that day.

We got into the car and drove up into the foothill part of the mountains, towards the town of Evergreen. The wonderful thing about mountain driving is the long passages between towns that are filled with nothing but nature – extreme, raw nature. It's part of why I love taking drives as much as I do.

We drove for quite some time and after following the same road for many miles, I spent much of my time enjoying the beautiful trees, the rocks and mountain edges jutting out into the canyon, and the random wildflower poking its way up and through the rocky, sandy soil breaking free from the depths of winter's grasp. I had neglected to take notice of the ever so quiet and peaceful creek that ran alongside the road the entire way. Most mountain roads are trailed on the parallel by a water source of some kind, be it a creek, river or raging waters. However, what struck me so strange was how quiet and demure this river seemed to be. It wasn't lyrically loud or running amok with white waves crashing against the mountainside and the boulders in its path. No, this river was gentle and flowing, casual and partially hidden beneath the snow-capped ice formations hovering atop its surface. Little sections of flowing water could be seen from time to time, which is probably why I had failed to notice it amongst all the other beings who demanded themselves be seen.

But this beautiful little river did catch my attention because of its subtle nature. Unlike Oak Creek in Sedona, this river didn't want to be seen, not in the way some water beings want attention for their creations. Instead, it happily and lazily flowed about its business down the mountainside and into passing streams.

Immediately, upon taking notice, what I did not see was a specific river being. Instead, I clearly began to hear the dancing sound of water sprites singing in my head. The river water sprites sang a wonderfully beautiful tune:

"Twisting, flowing, running, slowing.
We follow the trail and path our ancestors built for us."

The river water sprites danced and sang their merry tune as they carried on about their energy duties. I knew there was a water being about, as the sprites themselves do not create the energy of the river itself, but spend their time cleaning and assisting in their joyful way. However, this river being had no desire to communicate or even to really be seen. Instead, he was busy at work doing what rivers do best – creating life with water.

No man ever steps in the same river twice, for it's not the
same river and he's not the same man.
- Heraclitus

All river beings have a similar purpose of creating a life with water, but each of them expresses it in their own unique way, as an individual creator. We cannot make them want to talk to us, nor would this be of a very smart design to do so, and when we find ones who are willing, engaging with them is a very wise thing to do. But no matter whether we begin a relationship with the actual creator being, we can still enjoy the glory of the creation and the beauty of what has manifested, and allow ourselves a connection in that way.

Never does nature say one thing and wisdom another.

- Juvenal, Satires

LAKES

Lake beings vary as much as ocean beings based on where the lake is, how close it is to people, what kind of water it has, and the kinds of plants, animals and other beings that live in or nearby. I went to visit Lake Ballinger near my home in suburban Seattle to experience the type of beings who choose to live and work in a very densely populated area. When I arrived at Lake Ballinger, I found several people laughing and playing, many ducks and their babies enjoying the water and low-flying birds swooping across the top of the lake. I sat quietly, engaging in the water itself and watching the activity ensue. I wasn't sure if the lake beings would attempt communication with so much activity, but as I always am, I was pleasantly surprised when three water beings walked across the lake and approached me. The three beings were definitely water-specific beings, although they were guardians of the lake area as well. One specific being had a very distinct energy, highly reminiscent of the 1970's. While talking to him, I could see flashes of light, colors, and energy patterns that represented that time period in our history. I did not inquire about why he exuded that energy, but I later learned that the 1970's were an important time period for this area of Washington, including Lake Ballinger. The other two beings did not exude the same energy. They felt and looked more akin to other water beings.

As I sat on my bench, I greeted them with a hello and the water being with the 70's aura spoke with the other two supporting and honoring him and what he had to say:

"Welcome to our little lake. We welcome visitors of all kinds to come and enjoy the beauty that we have created here. This lake is for all to enjoy, not just the persons living directly around it. Yes, there are island dwellers (nonphysical beings who live on the little patch of land right in the middle of the lake only accessible by boat or swimming) *who provide guidance and protection for the animals living amongst the trees. Welcome, welcome! Our lake is a lake of beauty amongst denseness. We provide an alternate reality for those seeking refuge from the daily grind. Our lake is peaceful and serene and destined for cleansing the auras of those who come to heal here. Water is a great healer, all water, no matter the location. Yes, this place is for healing. You can swim or float or smell or taste or just sit by the side of the water as it penetrates your core to allow freshness to flow in. This is our purpose. No other. We are here for peace and refuge amongst the chaos and insanity that comes with city dwellers. Please accept our invitation to join us in love and peace within the water. Come join us and play."*

The lake beings also expressed that there were many beings on this lake, not just the three of them. They were the spokesbeings for the lake community of non-physicals. It was clear their message was one of guidance and invitation to come and enjoy the healing waters or just simply to allow the lake to fill you. Their message and the feeling they exuded was quite different than lake beings found primarily in natural settings.

Last year, I visited a unique lake in northern Washington called Diablo Lake. This particular lake is unique because the silt that runs down the mountainsides in which it rests runs into the water and turns it turquoise blue. It's breathtaking to be driving along the highway among many beautiful lakes and mountains and out pops this lake that looks like liquid turquoise. Animals and fish predominantly do not live in this lake, nor do they drink from it, yet there were two lake beings watching over and guiding the waters and the other life that lives there. Keep in mind, that many times simply because we do not see life as we know it living and moving, it does not mean there is no life at all. This is what they had to say:

"Yesterday, we saw a blanket of snow upon our beingness and yet our vast experience does not change from day to day. We cleanse, we purify, we canvas the area with our energy. We continue our pursuit of creation to create once again. Our purpose is not for you. Our purpose is to be here in."

Another excellent example of a lake with little apparent life to the naked eye is Soap Lake in eastern Washington. Soap Lake is a very unique lake filled with high levels of minerals and layers upon layers of silt, mud clay and more. There are no fish in Soap Lake and the salinity has been tested to be ten times greater than that of the ocean, yet there are small bugs that live happily in the lake in these extreme conditions.

As with all water, Soap Lake has a water being that oversees its water. I noticed a slight difference from many of the other water beings I had talked to in that this water being was distinctly feminine. She had a feminine outline with long flowy liquid hair, feminine features, and wore a liquid gown. This was unique because most water beings come across very neutral in energy gender or with a hint of masculinity. She almost looked like a water angel without wings. I asked my guides about why this water being was so distinctly feminine and they explained that because her primary job was the protection and regulation of healing waters that her energy would come across more feminine than other water beings as she spent her time nurturing, healing, and helping others to receive. I spent three days with the Lady of the Lake, as I came to call her, swimming in the alkaline waters and watching the water bugs swim and dive. She came to visit each time and this is what she had to say:

"Yes, I am the lady of the lake and I live here breathing the purity of this water into your world. My job is to help those who come for my assistance and purify their bodies and their needs and cleansing pain. I watch over my brethren, you who need my waters and I offer my assistance in earnest of what you ask for. I cleanse

and purify your hearts and your soul bodies with my waters, so come and please enjoy my offerings. Soap Lake/Smokiam Lake was created as a universal need to clean yourselves of energetic impurities. There are three lakes of this kind all along the same plane with a universal shifting power, but our need is changing and few come for my help. I cannot run dry for those who protect me as I protect you. My message is one of hope on your planet. There is hope and healing easily accessible through earthly means if you so choose to ask for it. Come to my waters and bathe with light in your heart and heal your body from toxins and impurities. We wait for you. You do not need us, though we can provide relief from physical existence through nurturing your soul body. Come to us and enjoy our waters. We will not run dry. My final message is that of great despair: please do not. The planet is not in such a crisis as has been said. We need your help as we are all one on this planet, but do not despair so greatly. Choose wisely instead. Clean yourselves and you clean the earth."

Her message, as well as the messages of all the lake beings, no matter how unique and varied, rings true for anyone who visits or connects with those important waters, no matter if they are man-made or of the nature variety. What we can learn from them teaches us that life may not be apparent around or in the water itself, but the life inside the water is equally important.

The cure for anything is salt water – sweat, tears, or the sea.

– Isak Dinesen

OCEANS

Ocean beings have a very special message for people to hear, especially the ocean beings that live near populated areas. If you were to travel far out into the ocean and seek out the beings that live there, the message would be more universal and less people-specific. The work and infinite variety of ocean beings can be applied to several different categories, though for introductory purposes, I will focus on three: ocean beings near populated areas, distant ocean beings, and ocean wave beings.

In every outthrust headland, in every curving beach, in every grain of sand there is the story of the earth.
- Rachel Carson

OCEAN BEINGS NEAR POPULATED AREAS

Ocean beings near populated areas have a specialized interest in being connected to human beings, animals, and plant materials that produce specific energetic and physical results for the human population. Ocean beings of this nature prefer to create energy that ties natural aspects of the energy to physical aspects of our culture, as well as promote rapid succession of changes to maintain and sustain human and worldly needs. Ocean beings near populated areas are highly attuned to human intricacies and communicate with them often, whether the humans know it or not. They desire an established relationship with the humans in their area and they work to maintain a positive relationship between the needs of the earth and ocean, as well as those of the human and animal populations.

Ocean beings predominantly cleanse and purify the ocean water through energetic and physical means. They work in conjunction with the animals of the ocean who also strive to maintain clean, pure water energy. Ocean water beings that reside near heavily populated areas work to preserve a synchronized harmony with all the inhabitants of that particular area by use of the water's energy. Some areas are more highly charged because of the sheer amount of energy being poured into it by the water entities, humans, animals and plant life, as well as Mother Earth and all the other beings. Other areas are less activated because of decreased animal life, fewer humans with interest and attention, and difficulty in maintenance of plant life. Still, there are ocean beings working to cleanse and purify the area, the water, and the energy. The ocean beings exist in all areas of the water and with assistance, the area becomes a place of great beauty and significant energetic magnitude.

In places of high human population and excessive negative energy output due to pollution, dumping, negativity, poverty with anger, hatred or bitterness, fighting and war, destruction, and more, the ocean beings work to preserve the water's integrity with mostly a neutralizing effect. Most of the energy simply goes to equalizing the outpouring of harsher, more destructive energies. The ocean beings maintain and exist for the water, but they will work conjointly with those seeking to assist them in their work. Water of any kind is an amplifier and if the inhabitants of a specific area are calling for a specific type of energy, this energy will become amplified. The water itself is the amplifier and will broaden the energies of any given area and the outpouring that goes directly into the water. The ocean beings work to harmonize the water of the ocean, but they cannot deflate or magnify the energy poured into the water by the nearby inhabitants. Just as any souls who wish to magnify an event can do so simply by magnifying their sheer numbers and their own energy, the ocean beings will work in harmony with any other being who matches their cleansing and purifying pursuit.

Ocean beings are not the ones responsible for any event or occurrence in which the water engages in dramatic episodes. This comes directly from the mass energy transferred into the water by the nearby inhabitants and their thoughts, actions, expressions, ideas, and basic auric details. The water just amplifies what it experiences. Changes in the behavior of the water must come from the inhabitants, not from a plea to the beings that maintain the water. There can be requests for assistance through cleansing, purifying or simply toning down an event. This can be done with great love and honesty towards the ocean beings and Mother Earth, as well as the ocean itself. All natural events can be dissipated with respect and care, if only the attention and focus returns to that.

Ocean beings near populated areas have many, many, many messages and inspirations for anyone seeking their wisdom. Their messages focus on love and caring for one another in harmony with the water and both land and water inhabitants. They also offer to help us purify our bodies of unnecessary energies and discontented cellular satiation. A brief call to the ocean beings will bring them to your aid and in return they will ask for a simple outpouring of positive, loving energy to the water of your area. You don't even have to live by the ocean to call an ocean being into your experience, nor do you have to be in the presence of the ocean to experience them. Ocean beings near populated areas are highly attuned to working with people anywhere and they want to harmonize the existences of all entities on earth.

When I called in the ocean beings for the first time, I opted to do so in my home, even though I live close to ocean water. When they showed up, it was in droves. My room filled with light, fluid ocean beings too many to number. They expressed an appreciation immediately for someone willing to work with them and share their knowing with others. They offered assistance graciously and I accepted with great love. They then had a message to share:

"We work homogeneously because our purpose is singular. We offer love, hope, inspiration, and duty to those who seek to help us in our work. We work to purify the ocean waters for all to enjoy and exist in harmony with one another. The water is a mainstay of all life on earth and it is quite necessary for all of us to find respect and honor that which gives us life on our earth. We offer a potential for true cleansing and purifying all the waters of the world and enter into communion with the water's knowing to allow it to become as we are, that which we are. We wish for the water to enter us, into our beingness, and through this entrance we are allowed an insight into the world of what exists below the water's edge. We can all offer the water our hope, love, joy and gratitude for the life-giving opportunities we are afforded. Even for us, we are given life by the water's energy and purity. It spurs our desire to create. It gives us the ability to manifest, as we use the energy to enliven all that live nearby the water's edge. Our water is our gift into life-beingness. It is no more physical than we are not physical. Water is simplistic and giving, it also receives from many sources and yes, it will amplify whatever you give to it, unless you request it take something away from you. This water can do easily. The ocean moves frequently, but all water does this. Water is all sources, up, down, side to side. There is no greater source than water, not even air. Water is our creator and what creates for us. This has been forgotten over much of your time. Water is taken for granted and used without care or gratitude. The water will give you true life, if you accept its gifts as more than givingness. Gifts

are presents unto the future and past of all things. There is much memory in water and this memory is key to knowing all that is offered on this planet. Take this key and open the door into greater understanding. The water will tell you stories and truths you have known before. This will be a great gift to you, should you like to receive it. There are many places to receive such gifts, but each will share a new tale, as you are truly made of only three things: earth, water, and sky. These are the places to find your lore and in finding yourself you will know us. Share your love, gratitude, respect and honor with the water and the water will become your greatest friend. Share your anger, fear, betrayal and worry with the water, and it will show you your greatest enemy. Give the water your pain and it will cleanse you, but in return you must accept a cleansing. Constant sharing of one type of energy will only protect you from growing. This does not allow for greater knowledge and the secrets that lie in the ocean will stay there. Raise your vibrational score and the ocean will meet you on the rise. Do not delay if you want to experience more of what has already been and what will always be. You are your own maker of your own story, but all stories are each of ours. This is the water's tale."

The message from the ocean beings ceased, but they stayed to energize my body and my beingness with the most beautiful power and filling of source. I could feel myself vibrating all over and as there were so many of them, it was coming from every direction. I began to pulsate faster and faster, as though it was becoming cyclic. I could feel the energy racing in waves across me. They then told me to rise up vibrationally and allow myself to feel all of what they were sharing with me. I could feel an expansion of myself, a growing within. It was such a calming and reassuring feeling that I did not want it to cease. What an amazing gift they truly are.

Either you decide to stay in the shallow end of the pool
or you go out in the ocean.

- Christopher Reeve

DISTANT OCEAN BEINGS

Distant ocean beings are beings who work to preserve and procure the ocean and its inhabitants from pollutants, ill-factors, and other non-beneficial organisms who inhabit the waters causing chaos, energetically and otherwise. Distant ocean beings prefer the title of cleansers or purifiers. They work to procure their environment so all inhabitants of the sea are allowed an equal chance to survive and strengthen themselves and the water's core. Distant ocean beings allow great waves of energy to pass through the ocean's outer layers into the deep core of water filtration systems far below the surface. These ocean creators work to produce visual results in terms of light energy, wave creations, and water production deep in the sea. Each ocean being has a specific area to master and a specific task to be held. These tasks can range from earth purifiers with water enhancements to water fluctuation creators that preserve the uppermost layer's integrity.

Distant ocean beings work cohesively with moon creators to promote free movement in the water thereby allowing greater access to the sea life. They also move the energy from place to place which gives all sea life equal opportunity to benefit from each individual ocean being's experiences. The water is cleansed and purified manually through energetic means and then the water is moved physically with waves and wind elements. There are many, many distant ocean beings continually working to preserve our precious water source, which creates life and sustains all living things.

Distant ocean beings are most easily connected to off shoreline quite a distance and they are easy to engage with, albeit brief, as chatting is not their primary desire. I first met distant ocean beings on a cruise I took to Alaska. During the segments of open water, I could see and experience the work of the distant ocean beings as they generated new life and recycled energy forms into new creations of living matter and energetic presence.

"We the ocean beings of distance and purity like to procure our presence with hard work and energy sources that allow new access to old regimes of energy matter and form. We like to move the energy and sway it into cleansing the world and its water source. The water is very precious as it maintains all life in physical form in many, many ways. The water here needs desperate cleansing from ocean pollutants as well as ocean-human energy interactions. The energy here is malluted and needs new forms to create new life. Life has not stalled as we are always maintaining it. The animals of the ocean world also work to procure the energy of it. The dolphins and whales and fish are particularly helpful in these areas as they move closely to the energy of the earth and its other inhabitants. Dolphins like to play and their energy is one of clearing harsher energies. Whales like to swim and create new life with their energy. And the fish like to move and thrust the earth's energy into the water. This happens often and the energy of Mother Earth is quite purifying to water forms. We do not use Mother Earth energy to cleanse. We use light sources and energy matter to create new energy forms and energy wave patterns that move through the water and expel any misguided water energy. We prefer to work in one area and maintain that area constantly, although some of us move from location to location. We work in sync with one another always, as the energy is constantly interconnected no matter where the energy exists. Some of us work stronger than others as necessity calls for it and we provide new forms of energy particulars (matter) when called for to release,

cleanse, and purify. We enjoy our work very much and we look forward to human interaction. Some of us never meet humans although the boats are a nice change of pace as the energy changes when humans enter. This is different for us and we enjoy it. Animals provide much more assistance than do the humans, most of the time. We prefer our anonymity in our work although experiences from others are always welcome. This is what we do. We speak homogeneously mostly, as our work and aspect on this world is quite similar. We prefer a life of quiet grace and procurement of the waters. We enlist help from those willing to give it and we will present ourselves to anyone that asks for our help and is willing to assist with theirs. We can help cleanse and purify all water, including that of your physical body, which we understand to be quite significant and quite damaged. You do not love your water or the water you inhabit. This causes great discourse in your physical existence. Many of you are beginning to understand the significance of purifying the water with the energy of love and life, but few do it daily. This is what we do, but we do it for the ocean. We infuse the ocean with love, life and purity of Source energy. This renews the water's energetic makeup and assists it in assisting other energetic forms. The energy of water is life-giving, but one must receive that energy to be enhanced by it. We recharge the energy so it recharges you. It is symbiotic. All nature is symbiotic. Water is a source of purity and cleansing."

After the distant ocean beings finished their message, they infused the water of my physical body with love, life, and purity of Source energy and it was an amazing feeling. My entire body began to tingle all the way from my head to my toes and I could feel energy moving in a way that I can only describe as "zinging."

The distant ocean beings have provided all of us with a great insight on how the water in everything is easily renewed with simple basic energy infusion. This can be done in a myriad of ways and there are scientists now exploring how thought and words infused into water produce fantastic ice crystals simply by focusing on one thing - love.

Nature is my manifestation of God.
I go to nature every day for inspiration in the day's work.
I follow in building the principles which nature has used
in its domain.

- Frank Lloyd Wright

OCEAN WAVE BEINGS

On my cruise to Alaska, in the evening and late into the night, I would spend a significant amount of time just sitting on my verandah and watching the water and the waves. Most of the time our water adventure was quite smooth and calm, but on one particular evening while we were out to sea, the waters were a little choppy and there were lots of waves to be seen in the darkness. As I watched the waves cresting and falling, I could see wave beings riding on the wave. Some wave beings were engaged in an activity that looked like surfing; others were just standing and working on top of their wave. Wave beings have a purpose of creating change and flow. They are not always present, such as when the water is calm, and as we have all seen in documentaries, some are much more dramatic in their work than others. I asked one friendly wave being if he would like to speak with me and if he had a message for you:

"We, as water beings of the waves, surf and play upon the ocean top to create a place for healing waters through change and alternate flow. We make new pathways and we heal with lightness. You see the white upon the water's edge and know that we are there working our special magic to cleanse the earth. I have no message for you except to change with the flow as we do. Change your thinking, change your bodies, flow with the rhythm that is life and allow change to come quickly to you. We will work with you in play, but our primary work is solitary even from one another. We work in harmony only in that we work close to one another. Each wave being has their own agenda to play with, some are

destructive - to you - and others just play and change the rhythm. We have our work and you have yours. That is our message."

This wave being's message was short and sweet as are many messages from water beings who have minimal contact with human beings. Many prefer it that way, as their work is solitary and individualized. I have found that water beings of any kind that live and work closer to humans tend to have a greater desire to communicate and work with us in unison. Beings of any kind that do their work further from people tend to be less communicative and more surreptitious. This does not mean they don't want to talk with us, but that their message may be shorter and they may simply have less to say. Nature beings are just like us. If this can be hard to understand, equate it to human beings. Those who tend to live in or near cities tend to be very social, outgoing, enjoy other's company and love to have fun with other people. Those who tend to live high up on a mountaintop alone may tend to be quiet, reserved, aloof, and not much of a talker. There are those of us who enjoy and want to be with others and those of us who don't. This doesn't mean that anyone's work is less important than another's, but that their work is just carried out differently in an equally beautiful way.

We ourselves feel that what we are doing is just a drop in the ocean. But the ocean would be less because of that missing drop.

- Mother Teresa

MYSTICAL SEA BEINGS

Meeting the mystical sea beings is a perfect example that you can meet a nature being anywhere, anytime. I happened to be in my backyard doing some visioning about water, the ocean and the seas, when I noticed a water being near the top of my shed. I greeted the being and he approached me, eventually placing himself next to me on my bench swing. Even if I think I know what kind of being a particular entity is, I always ask them for confirmation and clarification. Having not met a mystical sea being previously (and quite frankly at the time, not even knowing what a mystical sea being was, only that my guides told me to include a chapter in this book), I was a little surprised when the water being announced it was a mystical sea being. He told me he had a message for me and wanted to talk, it could not wait. I left my seat and my cats outside and came in to write down his message.

First, he wanted to explain what mystical sea beings are and what their purpose is:

"We have a singular purpose of cleansing Earth properties within our sphere. We cleanse and purify much like other water beings, but we use - magic, shall we say. It is not magic as you think of magic, but for lack of a better word, that is what I shall call our abilities. We cleanse properties and areas in need of deep healing.

We have come and gone many times and we are here again to protect precious waters of the impurities being placed upon them energetically, physically and man-ually. Yes, man is contributing, obviously. However, what you may not know is that other entities are contributing as well. Energetic beings, physical beings, and other nonphysicals alike are contributing to a decline in earth energy by using life force without replacing it. We are here, again, to clarify that energy. You can learn to heal the planet of your own accord, yet most of you do not. You choose only to take and not reapply. This causes the discord. In centuries past, even millennia, and considerably beyond that back and forth, there have been gaps in energy structure that needed cleansing and we have come "before" to do such healings. This time, again, we wish to teach you to reapply using your wisdom combined with our tools. It shall be easy, if you apply the knowledge. Our knowledge, some call ancient, we call universal. It works in many places, many times, many ways if used correctly and often. It shall be easy to learn, again, if that is what you all wish. We are here to teach, for if you no longer need us, we shall go and not have to come again to cleanse and purify that which you can do for yourselves. There are many of us, all around your globe working 'round-the-clock' as you say, to prevent further catastrophic energetic events. These are not catastrophic in the way you think of them in terms of natural event; they are energetic events of highs and lows involving energy spikes and dips in the energy system. Mostly there are dips now from overuse and not reapplying. We wish for your help in speeding this recovery and our departure. We will work with you quickly, if you choose to learn."

As the mystical sea being was telling me about his work, I could feel an itching spreading over my body and odd sensations that kept distracting me from focusing. At first, I thought there were mosquitoes or gnats nearby, but the mystical sea being told me that he was doing the cleansing and purifying on me that he does for the earth.

"The Earth called us here this time, as in times past. We have expressed ourselves before to others and some have tried to work on planetary energy for the benefit of others. There are others working on it right now, but in slower, less progressive ways. We have new ways to reteach you. Once, you all knew. Now, we will share it again in hopes you shall take the lead and begin to reapply the energy as you use it. In all systems, relationships of energy must be symbiotic in order to be sustained. We have developed a method for this energy exchange and it is easy and simple with no time lost. You must do this to balance the energy. Little to no work must be done to maintain it. It is a constant ongoing maneuver to maintain what already exists in the balance. The Earth will do her part. You can do yours, now. Yes, you will see significant changes if these tools are put to use immediately. We will always be available for your assistance. We will always come. Yet there is no reason if you can do it yourselves and it is so easy too.

"First, we will tell you more about mystical sea beings. Mystical sea beings first arose out of a need for shifting energy patterns on planets without life forms where energy was only moving in one direction. These directions could be in-going or out-going, yet never neutral. We came to balance their systems. Many times we didn't need to stay long, only as long as it took. We have gone by many names - mystical sea creatures, land dwellers, earth movers, words not in your language for other planets and realms, yet our mission is still the same: to heal energy patterns gone awry. Your energy system has been in need for much time, thus we have been here for longer than we usually stay in a system. There is much taking going on and little reapplying. This is why Earth called us here again.

"Many may wonder why we are sea beings and not of other form. We chose water because water is so easily moved and manipulated in terms of energy. Water is fluid energy in many, many ways and on this planet, it moves quickly and easily to change and shift energy patterns. However, we pull them into balance and you pull them out again. There must be equal maintenance upon Earth for us to leave. This you can do yourselves. We stress this to you because although we enjoy our work and our presence here is uplifting, you ultimately must make the change to maintain balance – we can only create temporary change.

"This is how you do it. Pray into the Earth as you are One with all life. That's it. Pray does not mean words or even thoughts,

no. Pray means to become one with and allow the energy to pass through to another, in this case, Earth. You may do this to a water source, into the land on which you stand, or into the sky up above. Many say they pray now and they send love and energy into the Earth. This is partially true. You do speak words and thoughts unto the Earth and you send it love and peace, but you do not pray unto it, into it. You must become one with it and understand that you and the Earth are the same. There is no difference between what is you and what is Earth or any other life form. By praying into the Earth, as One, you reapply the energy you have used into yourself as well as into others. This is quite simple. It can be done without even a thought. It can be done without time. It can be done without effort. Simply understanding and acknowledging what it means to pray into the Earth will begin the process that will unfold into behavioral and energetic patternizations. You will see changes, but not if you do not see you are one with all life. Not just in energy, what you call God-consciousness – there is more you are in equivalence to the Earth. There is much, much more. And this you shall discover by praying into the Earth, daily to begin and eventually always. This is our message for you - wait, I have more. We ask a request of you: spend time in yourselves as you pray into the Earth. This you will see will lead to a greater understanding of what we mean when we say you are One. Some understand its true meaning, but not many, yet. We see great understanding coming and this is the beginning. Pray into the Earth often, and soon, always. You will feel your energy clear. Quick and immediate. This is my message and our request for you. We are here to help you understand more. You may call upon us anytime you like by simply asking for us or praying into the Earth."

As the mystical sea being was readying to leave, I did not want to question his message, but I had to ask him why he chose the word 'pray' because there is so much associated and attached to that word. He said to me, *"Yes, it is 'pray.' You will come to understand."* After his departure, I sat and thought about what he had said and three things occurred to me about this message:

"Pray into the Earth as you are One with all life."

1) There is no comma after 'Earth' which would significantly change the meaning to the sentence and I was later told that was intentional.

2) The definition of pray according to The New Lexicon Webster's Encyclopedic Dictionary of the English Language (1989) is:

Pray *(prei) v.i. to enter into spiritual communion.*

3) The words chosen by the mystical sea being are meant to be *instructions*, not a description of who or what we are (see revelation #1). Pray into the Earth *as though you are One with all life*, not because you are.

Mystical sea beings are creatures and entities who wish to supply us with the information necessary to reallocate undesired source energy into positive source supply. This can be done anywhere, anytime and doesn't cost anyone a thing except a little focus and direction. It will enhance your ability to connect with nature and earth, as well as other people, plants and animals. Reapplication of source energy is necessary for our survival as physical entities on earth – and there is as much giving in receiving, as there is receiving in giving.

A few minutes ago every tree was excited, bowing to the roaring storm, waving, swirling, tossing their branches in glorious enthusiasm like worship. But though to the outer ear these trees are now silent, their songs never cease.

- John Muir

STORMS

True storm beings tend to work in groups of four. They can carry smaller groups or larger groups, but on average they will clump in groups of four depending on what is needed in an area. The group of four typically includes a cloud being, wind being, water being, and an energy being. There are specific types of beings within each of those categories and depending on the situation, there will be different ones for different purposes.

Cloud beings are pretty self-explanatory except that there are many, many types of clouds formed in many, many types of ways.

Wind beings that travel in storm packs tend to be more purposeful and more dedicated to the issue at hand than, say, a breeze being. Just as with any other physical form, there are non-physicals who provide a lot of energy and those who provide a smaller, more gentle amount, and those who change based on what they feel like or when they want to exert more or less.

Water beings that join storm packs tend to be rain beings, although there are an infinite number of other types of water beings who also work towards causing universal change within a storm.

Energy beings in storms come in a variety of forms including lightning beings, electrical energy beings, thunder beings, and more. The energy beings focus on jumpstarting the energy in the storm and forward motion of the entire pack. They tend to be the leaders and directors of the storm packs with their particular cause in focus while they are working and creating movement.

Storm beings do not always travel together for their existence. Some do, yet others come together for a new experience or a group experience. For example, think of a rally for peace. There are those who run the rally, directing it, instructing what to do and when, and rallying people to join them. They are the leaders and those who really love it, spend their lives doing it. Then there are individuals who choose to join the cause for a week, a month, a year. And then there are those who join the rally for a day and then go back to working in their office cubicle on a regular basis. It is the same for storm beings. There are those who like to cause change, some want to be a part of the change, or others who simply watch the change and they all do it in an infinite number of ways.

It is better to have less thunder in the mouth and more lightning in the hand.

– American Indian Proverb

THUNDER BEINGS

On a recent trip to the Grand Canyon, a friend and I stopped along the South Rim to see the various sites. As we were about to complete our journey, we came upon the last viewpoint before we left for the day. My friend and I walked around the area just taking in the beauty that is the Grand Canyon and all its energy and glory and watched as an impending storm was rolling across the canyon. My friend and I watched this dark, ominous cloud move slowly towards our viewpoint. We watched with awe, as this dark cloud was right at our height from where we stood and brought with it an immense amount of power and energy, particularly for the small size of the cloud. The cloud was heavy and low and in it came four beings working their special form of energy change. There was a thunder being, a wind being, a rain being, and a lightning being in this small and powerful storm cloud. My friend and I didn't stay long as this cloud carried a lot of power and it was headed for our direction. The thunder being began to speak with these words of warning:

"If you see us, run for your covers because we bring highly charged life and energy to your earth. We wish no harm, nor peace, but change and for life on your planet. Our work is one for those who wish deep, profound change and as though it may seem devastating in that time, we work towards life and courage to see what can come from what you call destruction. Our power is one

of courage and life-giving. We have come to clear the way here in the canyon. To clear the pollution and energy disrupters quickly and abruptly. Much pollution clouds the canyon. We work to heal that here. In other places, thunder comes for change and devastation of what once was. We dance and dance and dance until you see what it is we have come to have you hear. Hear our roar as we call upon you for change. Use our wisdom, for it is deep and with many ancestors. We call upon you for change. Change in your ways, change in your mind, change in your heart for that is where your power lies. Behest our warning to find your change and make a new way for we shall come to assist you if you cannot find your way."

Geniuses are like thunderstorms.
They go against the wind, terrify people, cleanse the air.
                                                    -Soren Kierkegaard

LIGHTNING BEINGS

Lightning beings are energy beings made of current and electricity designed to surge through the sky and create epoch changes internally and externally in all paths they cross. Lightning beings are specialized in that they are not like other energy beings, which essentially come in great varieties and multitudes, for lightning beings work directly from the sky, whereas other energy beings work directly from the earth and earth's energy.

Lightning beings like to work their specialized magic across the sky in zigzag patterns to create pools of electrical changes. Using a zigzag pattern, initially they strike out with force and energy and then pull back for a short period of restitution, only to strike out again. This pattern is repeated with lightning strikes and energy chords to allow for the change to occur within the movement. Too much change can prevent the change from happening by not allowing it to be processed smoothly. This all happens instantaneously, yet from the lightning beings perspective, it is simultaneous and there is a point for restitution of the process of change happening. Restitution is necessary to allow the beings receiving the change to balance themselves before more change happens, quickly. It doesn't require time - none of us really need time. It does however require patience and aptitude for perseverance to the next level. This is what the strike pattern allows.

In an unusual display, filled with grace and power, from my home one night, I witnessed a beautiful electrical storm that eventually turned into a thunderstorm. I turned off all the lights and the television and just watched the lightning beings along with the cloud beings create and manifest the most glorious display I've seen in quite awhile. I asked the lightning beings if they would like to share a message and they immediately responded with a "We're too busy!" statement. It seems that while they are working, they are acutely involved with their trade. They agreed to visit later and share their story.

The next day, I spent much time thinking about them and the beauty of their display and how unusual it was for our geographic location. I had just returned from a trip a few weeks prior to southern Washington near the coast and residents there told me it was quite common to see electrical storms overhead. This made me wonder why they had traveled so far north this time and joined with the other storm beings to create a full thunderstorm. In the storm, I could see cloud beings hard at work, thunder beings making their noise creations, and rain beings waiting to drop their load upon the earth and sky. As I waited for the lightning beings to give me a message to share, I could feel the energy around me and my body surging with electrical force. It wasn't particularly powerful (thank goodness!), but it was incredibly present. I could feel the little hairs on my arms and body standing on end and I could feel the presence of a lightning being waiting patiently for me to perceive them. This lightning being's energy was much more subdued from the night before and slowly I could see him come into focus. He cast a yellow white glow with sharp, jagged edges emanating from his center. He waited patiently in my presence for his opportunity to share this message:

"Last night was a great work of art. We played unlike we have played before. There has been much travel and time and space to allow us to move to your location and put on our show. We did come for change, but we like to have fun too. Our work is our fun. This is true. We played in a new way last night for you and for others to see that there is change coming here to Seattle. There is a change on the front, on the air, in the wind. We wish to be a part of the journey and so we came. Last night was an offering, a warning of what is to come. Nothing must change; all is well in what we do. We find ourselves looking for more motivation and opportunities to create something new and here there is something new, a new opportunity.

"We wish to offer all readers an opportunity to work with us. We are not to be feared. We are not to be loathed. We do not harm those who ask for our assistance. There are some who get caught in the aftermath of their decisions and this may look as though it were our fault, yet it is not. This is the desire they have chosen without realizing it, maybe so. We offer an opportunity for unrest to be met with new challenges, new insight, new opportunities. We do not sit around and wait for change, we are the change you seek. Seek us in your hearts and we will offer you growth and spiritual knowledge for the next step, the next level in your beingness. This is what we have to offer your readers, those who seek our assistance. We shall come and we shall strike into your hearts with an electrical impulse to make the changes you

desire. This can be done as much and as often as you ask it to be done until you are where you want to be."

I then asked the lightning being to infuse my heart with courage and reduce my fears. I could see the lightning being take aim with a bolt and send it straight to my heart. There was a slight pulsation and energy change that was very subtle. Then, I could feel the energy ooze out from my heart and into my body field. I asked for two treatments and was offered both, yet I could see how the restitution must still be made. I must still *choose* to make changes in that moment of pause. They can help lift and guide me with energy infusions, yet I must still be the one to accept the changes and allow for something new. I realized that no one can force us or do it for us, yet this beautiful, amazing lightning being was willing to offer me a subtle energy force to make that happen with an easier transition, a lighter beingness. I asked the lightning being why they want to assist us with our personal and global changes.

"Why? Why does a mother want to help its children? Because we love you as you are us and all things. We are all one and if we can help you achieve the peace you desire in your life with the tools we have, then why should we not? This is what we do. We bring about force and change. Yet, you are right. We cannot force you to change. We cannot allow for the change you are seeking without your permission to do so. You must be the key. We can help you

unlock your doors. We have a gift of light, power, and energy. These are things that are inside all of us. We want to help you bring them out into your focus. There are many of us to choose from and some of you will work with us, others will choose another being for assistance. We offer because we see the light of love inside all of all beings. This we wish to bring more of onto your earth. Peace will come from knowing this in your very being and this we can help you with. Allow us entrance and we will seek the answers with you. You are never alone in your journeys and there is always help available to you in many, many ways. Seek it if you wish and we shall help you grow."

Lightning beings love to work and play with people energetically. They will give you a charge if you feel you need one and they will provide understanding for the storms in your life that are to come to bring about change and everlasting influence for greater understandings. Lightning beings love to be nature's aspectual forms dancing across the sky and lighting the pathways to higher truths, greater connections to nature, and illuminating the clouds of change. Invite them in and allow their electrical abilities to charge your life, illuminate your heart and mind, and breathe fresh new life into your cellular memories. Lightning is a fantastic way to open up to higher channels of wisdom and spirituality with a direct connection between the circuits of your being and the wires of the universe. You will find great truths that come from understanding the "darker" sides of nature, the sides that are cast off into what we deem as foreboding or destructive. These sides allow us to ply into our true selves without fear of neglecting our physical selves. They allow us to peacefully choose an alternative to physical chaos or physical destruction by not allowing our true selves to shine (refer to the section in Chapter 2 on Energetic Earth Beings for more references on shining). These beings have often sought to help us and assist us in furthering our divine and natural education and yet we turn them into beasts of destruction and hopelessness. All nature beings have a blessed purpose and each is brought into our lives by how we call them.

It is not light that we need, but fire; it is not the gentle shower, but thunder. We need the storm, the whirlwind, and the earthquake.

- Frederick Douglass

A cloud does not know why it moves in just such a direction and at such a speed...It feels an impulsion...this is the place to go now. But the sky knows the reasons and the patterns behind all clouds, and you will know, too, when you lift yourself high enough to see beyond horizons.

– Richard Bach

CLOUDS

Cloud beings come in so many different forms and just as with all other beings, each has their own agenda and their own itinerary. Some work solo, others work in unison. Some work to build things, others just enjoy the moment. Cloud beings love to purify the air and gently, although sometimes swiftly, carry themselves across the sky. Cloud beings are highly transient and love to create images by carving shapes in the sky. Most cloud beings live within their cloud, yet they do not become nearly as overly involved in their physical creation as many other nature beings. This is due to their transient nature in that physical cloud forms dissipate and reform over and over and over again, allowing their non-physical counterpart to be much freer in their movements and choices. Cloud beings are builders and sightseers. Most cloud beings prefer to move air quickly and efficiently while they enjoy their existence and to bring new laughter to the air.

On a recent trip to Soap Lake in central Washington, I sat in the lake and gazed up at the beautiful clear blue sky. I noticed a rather large cumulus cloud working its way east and set my intent to seeing what type of cloud beings were working within the cloud. In that enormous cloud, there was a set of four beings working together to move it, guide it, direct it, and manage its size. Each cloud being had its own work to do and went about it in unison with the others. As the cloud made its way across the sky rolling and billowing its massive form, I connected with two of the cloud beings who were willing to share some insight into their lives:

"I guide, direct and motivate the cloud to move its form along the pathway. We four have come together to create a new cloud experience as many of us have worked solo for much of our existence. We chose a unified experience for the brevity and the newness. We do not have to choose it for long, yet some of us prefer unison over individuality."

"I work to maintain the height of the cloud as my primary job is to maintain and manage it. I am allowed to choose size and shape with respect to what my counterparts are creating. This is a new experience for me as I have chosen individual assignments prior. We mostly move and change the cloud into areas of need such as places in need of rainfall or shading. We work with many, many beings along the way whether we are individual or unified, such as rain beings, sunbeam beings, moonbeam beings to a lesser degree, air beings, wind beings, and more and more and more. There are so many to work with and in so many different ways. You will find many wonderful experiences as we have by engaging with all of them from time to time. I really like being with people. I have worked with people for millennia and I really like creating animals for people to see. That brings me great joy. Not all of us feel the same way, but I do. I like to be seen in the sky. The landscape is always quite beautiful from up here and I invite all of you to join

me on a cloud to see your life as we see it, from the sky. There is much more to be seen. Come join us. Be kind and ask first, as there are some of us who prefer to experience life individually, just as you do. We respect that as you do us. Thank you for seeking communication. It has been a nice change of pace. There is so little of that among inter-beings, cross-communication. Thank you for honoring us. Thank you for being here and doing your work. Thank you, thank you."

Just as with human beings and animal beings, there are nature beings who really enjoy communicating, some who enjoy it but have little to say, and others who do not want to communicate at all. Respect them as you would any other being and ask for communication. Trust what you hear if you have a being who prefers not to be touched or communicated with and seek out those who like to chat.

You will find something more in woods than in books. Trees and stones will teach you that which you can never learn from masters.

- Saint Bernard

ROCKS

Rock beings live within the rocks they inhabit and they inhabit them for longer than many of us can conceive of being in a body. Their space-time varies greatly from ours in that they move significantly slower than we do and have very little need to move great distances. I spoke with some rock beings once while sitting on a cliff and they described their experience of us in this way:

"You feel the need to move quickly and less efficiently. When we choose to move, which we do, we move with great care and ease. We choose our movements and we move in a different space-time than you as humans move. When you see small creatures move rapidly, they too are moving in a faster space-time than you choose to move. What we perceive of your movements in relation to ours is much like an insect to a human. One moves more quickly than another, by perception. In their reality, insects are moving at their own perceived slow space-time and humans move quite slowly. These are the layers of space-time and humans just perceive that we do not move –but we do. We can move quickly, but it can cause great damage to ourselves and others. You call them rockslides, we call them transfers. Sometimes we choose to create new rock beings by splitting ourselves and this can take many millennia; seemingly slow to humans, but quite fast for rocks. Our time is one of pace and ease and proficiency."

◆ ◆ ✿ ◆ ◆

Those who contemplate the beauty of the earth find
reserves of strength that will endure as long as life lasts.
- Rachel Carson

Many rock beings have inhabited the same existence for as long as the Earth has been in place. Some longer. They tend to feel very, very old. They have watched, guided, and overseen many things happen on our planet and because of their intense wisdom and longevity, they have much to say about life on this planet. However, I found that communicating with rock beings can be a bit challenging, as they are not as adept at communicating with people. Crystals are, but geologic formation communication tends to be more choppy and given in feelings and ideas rather than actual words. Mostly they say it is because people do not trust what the rock beings are sharing with them because what comes and the way it comes tends to be unique to rock beings. Many rock beings will show you images and past or future scenes, if you ask them as they are truly great storytellers, but most people have not chosen to communicate with them. Many rock beings have told me that cowboys were some of the best rock conversationalists because they spent so much time with them and like the rocks themselves, use few words if any to express an idea! When you sit with a rock being, allow anything – *anything* – you experience in as your message from them. It can be a feeling, an idea, a picture, or a one or two word answer.

A great way to begin communicating with the rock beings is to see their faces in the rocks themselves. Native Americans and many landscape and nature artists have painted pictures of them for centuries. Their faces change and move with their moods and what they are wanting to experience, including enjoying sunsets and watching birds fly. Rock beings tend to be easygoing, laid back, yet very intense in their purpose. Rock beings from several places have expressed to me that their purpose lies in holding our plane in existence. They work intensely with the Earth and earth beings to maintain our physical experience. Mother Earth is the being that holds all of the Earth itself as one and the rock beings are some of her oldest children. She speaks through them often and they hold a large amount of Universal wisdom within their beingness.

I spent some time with several rock beings along the Columbia River in southern Washington near Maryhill. As we began to communicate, it took some time for me to be able to put into words what I was getting from them and even then I had to ask my guides for extra assistance in forming words. Many times I was able to get a word or two. One particular rock being who chose to be the mouthpiece for the others kept making a yawing sound and I could see it trying to move its mouth in an attempt to form words. After watching this magnificent being working to communicate in a way that it felt I could understand, I told the rock being that it could communicate with me telepathically and immediately it stopped yawing and trying to form words. The words that came across were mostly singular, yet just as important. I highly recommend you spend time with rock beings to truly understand their unique way of communicating with us. It will make the following message all the more important, and understandable.

"Guardians.

Rock souls.

Long, long, long time. Millennia. More. Long.

Keepers. Seekers. Wisdom and truth.

Souls in this plane. We seek truth.

Universe one.

More to come. Long time more.

We seek truth as you. We hold true more of you. You. You. And we together as one.

Understand we're clear in you. You choose clarity in us. We help clear your way, The Way.

Guardians of all that is. Here. Now. More to come.

Seekers of peace and truth and One.

Now more than ever. We seek. We see. We know. We (all) are. Guardians of this earth. Our home planet. Yours. We seek peace. Truth. Oneness. And ask more. Of you.

We seek.

Truth."

Rock beings are quite easy to get along with and they will provide you with profound insight if you are patient and allow the messages to come as they give them to you. Rock messages can be difficult to understand, especially if you've never had an opportunity to converse with them. Most rock messages come in the form of a feeling or you may experience an energy pattern. Some rocks will give you very clear, concise information, while others work harder to communicate with you. Just allow them to give you information in the easiest way possible and feel free to express that to them. Many ancient cultures spent a great deal of time with rock beings and garnered a lot of wisdom from them. Our cultures today are not as adept at this and the rocks have not had as many opportunities lately. Be patient with how and what you receive and just experience it. Allow yourself to open up to their ancient wisdom, as well as their practical advice. They have plenty! Rock beings will share stories and scenes from their lifetimes, all you have to do is ask. Any way that you receive a connection to them will be the path chosen to allow you a straight connection to the divine.

I thank You, God, for this most amazing day: for the leaping greenly spirits of trees, and for the blue dream of sky, and for everything which is natural, which is infinite, which is yes.

- e.e. cummings

TREES

Tree beings are hands-down one of my favorite beings because I love trees and all that they stand for. Near my home, trees are abundantly available and unlike where I grew up in Denver, the trees in the Northwest are sky-high. Trees in the Northwest grow quite tall as if reaching straight for the atmosphere and the heavens above, particularly the evergreens. Trees, just like people, have distinct personalities and individual journeys. Trees provide a great source of life energy and are excellent for renewing lost or misplaced human energy. Trees are also intuitively connected to earth energy and Mother Earth.

Trees move in a slower space-time than we do, yet they can easily alternate and adapt to our space-time through movements of their branches, leaves, and flowers. In this slower space-time is how trees move their physical bodies and their root systems. Trees have been known to move themselves from one location to another, it just happens at a much, much slower pace similar to that of the rock beings. You may not actually see the tree moving itself along the ground, but over time, you may come back and find that the tree is now in a completely different location. Of course, some never move at all, but it has been noted by naturalists and hike guides that trees can and do move anywhere from a few inches to a few feet or even a few miles. Why? Why does anything move? To feel the movement, to create something new, to get what it needs.

There are limitless reasons why a tree being will make a challenging journey happen, but only the tree and the Universe knows that for sure and you will have to go and ask it for yourself.

The tree which moves some to tears of joy is in the eyes of others only a green thing that stands in the way. Some see Nature all ridicule and deformity, and some scarce see Nature at all. But to the eyes of the man of imagination, Nature is Imagination itself.

- William Blake, 1799, **The Letters**

Tree beings tend to express messages about peace and unity within oneself. Each tree being is as unique as each human being with its own journey and its own personality. Trees have a very neutral, balanced energy and they are cleaners of the earth and this plane. They clear away much of the energetic debris harbored and created by other plants, animals, and people, as well as nonphysical entities. Trees will give you the energy of stability, regeneration, and balance.

In my front yard are several evergreen and deciduous trees that I love to sit with and enjoy regularly. There are three tree beings who always provide me with a sense of comfort, release, and sweetness. I asked them if they had a universal message to share and all three responded with a resounding "Yes!"

The eldest of the three trees spoke first:

"Welcome, my friends to your introduction to our world and what we see. You will find there is much truth in all that is around you and what you are about to journey into. Find our hearts in yours and we will connect with you as one. You will want more and more as you realize truly how many beings are all around you, all the time. This is truth, whether you choose to experience it or not. Understand that our world is one of peace and harmony and we are here to offer you much knowledge about your world. We offer you blessings of freedom and joy and honesty in what surrounds you every day, everywhere. Listen for our cries to you as we ask you to do more with us. Seek out hope and hearth in our bosom that is Mother Earth. She will provide all that you need and all that you can ever ask for. Seek only that which will bring you hope and wisdom for all others are a waste of your time and energy. Believe what you hear and feel and seek not knowledge from those who deceive you with their trickery in false universalism. This one will provide you with honest and truth and integrity in your being. This is my message for you, dear ones. Seek us and we will meet you graciously with open arms into our lives for there is much wisdom in our knowing as is in yours. Together we can create beauty and gratitude all around us for it is already here. Seek us and all that

we offer to you daily. We wish you peace and harmony and hope in your lives with us by your window side. Love, hope and harmony are what we can provide. Peace be with all."

The middle tree offered this message:

"Yes, yes. I am here to offer you more in your life. We all ask for your forgiveness in yourselves. We know what has happened on your planet and we send you guidance every day about what can be done to undo the things you wish to have undone. We know you seek more and better truths and this we can provide. Yes, we can provide guidance to your lives as many beings among us do. Yes. Seek not false wisdom, but your own. You will know it when you seek it and we shall be there for you when you do. Yes. Seek not unknowings, but that which is already known. Yes. For this shall bring you the Light upon which you seek. Yes. And more and more and more to come, so it shall. Yes."

The youngest of the trees and the one located closest to my physical home had this to say:

"Oh my, welcome, welcome to our earthly treasures. This world is filled with more wisdom and knowledge than most of you realize in your daily lives. Come to us and seek our wisdom and we shall share it with you always. We have much to say and more to tell you than what we have room for today. Come to us and sit with us

under our broad leaves and branches and we will share stories of our lives and those who have lived among us. We seek those who seek truth and the wisdom of the ages we have to share. There is much to say and we wish for more visitors like you to come to us. We will provide you with knowledge and understanding of our ways and in return we would like a gift from you: your knowledge, your wisdom and your understanding. We wish to share our universal expansion with you. Come to us and offer yourselves. We want your stories, your heart and your home within. Come, come. I await you!"

The 'sister' tree beings that live near my home have shared wonderful messages to all and they provide a great overview of the desire tree beings have to communicate with us. As you are walking through your streets or in nature, feel the tree beings as they watch you and whether they want to communicate with you or not. Some will jump right out and want to share with you right away, others will be more reluctant. Remember that just as humans are having their own experiences, so are the tree beings.

Once, when I went hiking in a forest, I came upon a tree that had been sawed off midway up its trunk and the tree was covered in mushrooms and bugs and was splintered up and down all over each side. As I walked by this particular tree being, I began to reach out and touch it. Immediately, I received a message that said sharply, *Stop! Do not touch me, leave me be.* Clearly this tree being did not want to be touched, nor did it want to have communication with me. I made the mistake of not asking the tree's permission to engage with it, but it was not shy about letting me know how it felt. Just as you may meet a person or an animal that does not want to talk with you, any other type of being may also exhibit this same kind of behavior. Honor this request. Honor the Universe by not impeding upon another being's experience if they wish for you not to be there. We each have our own path to experience and all experiences are bringing about new life and new light to the Universal One experience, so honor that which may seem uninviting and unpleasant by letting the being have their experience their way.

Look at the trees, look at the birds, look at the clouds, look at the stars... and if you have eyes you will be able to see that the whole existence is joyful. Everything is simply happy. Trees are happy for no reason; they are not going to become prime ministers or presidents and they are not going to become rich and they will never have any bank balance. Look at the flowers - for no reason. It is simply unbelievable how happy flowers are.

- Osho

GRASS, PLANTS, SHRUBS, AND FLOWERS

I believe a leaf of grass is no less than the journey-work of the stars.

- Walt Whitman

GRASS

Grass beings are as individual as human beings, yet they work homogeneously to grow landscapes, meadows, and yards into varied creations. Grass beings feel quite a bit like water sprites and woodland sprites in that they have a playful, relaxed, joyous feel to their personalities as well as their individual work. They play and laugh and work determinedly towards achieving greater function in their physical being. Grass beings just love to create, create, create. They continually focus on growing their individual physical expressions into larger, better, taller, greener, huskier grass aspects. They are in a competition of sorts with other grass entities, particularly with those in close physical quarters. Grass entities love to outdo one another and although there are areas where grass may seem dead and gone, just wait and water the area for a period of time and the grass will return.

Grass is exceptionally hardy because the nature beings associated with them never give up. They stick close to their physical entities, although rarely inhabiting it, and work and grow either above or below the soil. The seeds just wait for the right opportunity, but they are far from dormant. Grass has been known to grow in the barren desert when there is enough rain.

Grass beings are kind and generous and they are exceptionally playful. Of course, not all grass beings will want to play, but on average if you encounter grass, you will encounter a loving, playful, almost celebratory being. These beings are true examples of entities who love who they are, what they are doing, and they never give up knowing that an opportunity will present itself for a re-emerging.

Grass beings have considerable patience simply because they know that time has no meaning for them. Seasons come and seasons go, rain comes and rain goes, but an opportunity will always show up eventually. It doesn't have to be today or tomorrow or even a decade from now. The conditions will manifest given the patience and the willingness to allow for it to come. This they believe to their core and they know the universe will conspire to dream a new dream, a new creation, a new outlet for their next existence. They feel no pressure, no need for anything to happen - it just does and they know it will. They are eternal and they know it.

Grass beings are excellent beings in which to learn patience and gratitude for a current existence. They will infuse you with their vitality and inspiration if you engage with them and allow yourself to receive their wisdom. They fashion themselves after the grass they are growing in physical form and they do not mind if you come to sit with them. The grass beings are not injured or disdained by someone or something walking on their physical creations, some actually prefer it. It gives them a challenge and a new opportunity. Grass is resilient and they simply ask that you respect their creations by not intruding on it without acknowledging them purely out of courtesy and respect for their work and their creation.

Whenever you mow, cut, or walk on any grass, know that there are nature beings working to realign that grass and remotivate it to become a new physical creation. Most grass beings do not mind the cutting, mowing, or stepping upon, however just as any other spiritual entity deserves kindness, respect and assuage of reticence, just make the action second-nature to acknowledge them and their creation before setting forth. This will imbue kindness and grace back to you from the nature beings who seek to inspire and connect with you.

"Listen to us. We hear you. We feel you in your presence walking upon our creations. We know you're kind in intention and blessings. Listen for us beneath your feet; we are always there, humming, singing, playing our tune of creation. Listen to us patter, listen to us glisten, listen for our tune of creation. Feel us when you walk barefoot knowing that we have created for you an experience of us. Touch the earth and the grass between, as we are creating a harmony in paradigm. Mingle your toes, run amongst

your fingers, trickle your water upon our bodies of earthen creating. We love to play; we love to laugh; and we wait for you."

Nature is full of genius, full of divinity...
- Henry David Thoreau

PLANTS

Plant beings are as varied as any nature being can be, simply because they offer a huge variety of knowledge, wisdom, and perspective from an earthly point of view. They grow, they create, they manifest, they produce, and sometimes they lay dormant until the opportunity arises again to begin growing, creating, manifesting and producing. Sometimes they just hold steady without big productions and other times you'd think they were mothers wanting nothing more than a million offspring. Each plant is different in what they offer and their creative purpose and each plant being is equally the same. They offer kindness, hope, wisdom, universal knowing and knowledge, earth properties, manifestation principles, and so much more solely based upon what type of plant being they are and what physical creation they are maintaining.

Plant beings can be transient and they sometimes move from one plant offering to another. Others prefer to stay with their plant species or in an area they helped manifest. Some plant beings, like water beings, move from plant to plant, creating and de-constructing over and over again for new experiences and new information. Plant beings are plant beings and what makes them different than grass, shrub or flower beings is how and what they produce. Plant beings are here to produce manifested desires. They want to produce production itself. They want to grow and cease to limit themselves to one type of existence. Of course they are like other nature beings and one could argue that flowers, shrubs, grass, trees, leaves and more are all types of plants, but plant beings can be pretty particular as to their type of existence. They don't want to be limited in how and what they create, but they do stay close to an essence of production.

Any botanist will tell you that trees and plants are not in the same category. There are millions of aspects of plants and an infinite number of plant beings. Please keep in mind that all nature beings are of the same essence, as we are. All of our spiritual makeup is the same, just with individual purpose and choices. Nature beings who choose a plant existence is just a category for this book. There are an infinite number of a multitude of beings. Don't limit yourself or your own understanding based upon what might be a plant or a tree or a shrub. There are unique attributes to all of them, but if you want to know more about a particular nature being, ask them yourself. They will give you the right answers. My limits in the descriptions are merely to emphasize the expansiveness that exists all around us and my wanting is to open you to the next possibility of connection with another spiritual being.

Having said that, plant beings are wonderful to expend energy with. They readily give and receive energy from universal sources and they are deeply and highly connected. They receive energy from the earth and return it to the sky. They enliven the area around them and they produce by-products that allow other beings to engage strongly in their own physical aspects. They are determined and like-minded, competitive with soft focus, and they seek to connect with other beings to enrich their own experiences. Plants make wonderful companions and they thrive on energy exchanges between care-takers and care-givers. They love to sing and engage in romantic expression. And they will always have a message for you.

"We have a message for you. Love us. Love all of us, as we love you too. We beings of plant origin prefer a life and existence close to people that love and cherish our existence. We enjoy the human experience as it relates to ours and we would like you to enjoy ours too. Plant experiences are social and abreast of all hardship. Most of us do not know struggle or lack of determination. We prefer a life of leisurely pursuit. We like to play amongst ourselves and we enjoy creating new avenues of enjoyment. We are always looking for something new and fun to try. We will experiment with right

creations and left givings. We explore and manifest blessed events of new makings. This is what we do. Create, create, create! We love to create. You may ask us for guidance in this area if you are preferring struggle now and wish for something else. This we can assist you with. Allow us to enter and assist you and we will! Thank you, thank you!"

Connecting with plants will be just like connecting with other nature beings. Plants that live in your home, on your property, or near urban areas will be more inclined to create a conversation with you, pending you have treated them well and with respect. They can be akin to their fairy cousins in that if you have not treated them with kindness or respect for their existence, they may not show themselves to you. If you have treated them with indifference simply out of ignorance to their true existence, they can be forgiving. If you have treated them with true malice, don't expect them to openly accept your invitations until you have amended your ways. However, I expect that if you have a truly malicious attitude towards plant life or nature itself, you probably won't be reading this book. Plants are highly forgiving as they are beings who are about giving and receiving in equal measure. They can teach you basic and advanced principles on receiving from all sources, nature and Divine. When you have engaged into dialogue with them, they will ask things of you, like removing dead branches or leaves. You do not have to treat them like royalty (unless they ask for that and you are willing to give it!), just treat them with respect and kindness and ask them what more you can offer them in their makings.

There are many rules and regulations about how often to feed or water a plant and with what, when and why. I say, ask the plant. They know what is best for their makings and they will tell you. When I am outside with my garden plants, I will ask them if they need water or if they need anything I can provide. Some say yes, others tell me they will need water in two days if it doesn't rain, etc, etc. I do this with my houseplants also. Some of my houseplants prefer a little bit of water every few days while others prefer more, but less often. Ask them. They will tell you. I treat my animal companions the same way. Instead of assuming I know what is best, I ask them and let them decide what is right for their individual experience. This provides for happy plants and pets, pending that is what they want to be.

I had a plant once that thrived and lived a very enjoyable plant experience until abruptly, its physical existence began to decline. I tried repotting it, feeding it, altering its water offerings, moving it, and continued on with such practices attempting to "save" it. I couldn't just let it die! I finally realized this particular plant being was done with its current plant experience and wanted to move on. I was attempting to force it to continue to exist, which is pretty much impossible. The plant being was probably getting a broad amount of information about the human experience simply by watching me and continuing with the charade for a short period of time. Eventually, I knew this plant was ready to let go and I could let go of it too. I didn't need to save it; I just needed to let it be what it was and what it was choosing. I finally learned to let it be who and what it wanted to be instead of what I wanted it to be. That can be a huge lesson for human beings. And this was taught to me by a beautiful, wise plant being.

That we find a crystal or a poppy beautiful means that we are less alone, that we are more deeply inserted into existence than the course of a single life would lead us to believe.

- John Berger

SHRUBS

Shrubs are fabulous beings to learn from. They are hardy, protective, magnificent and enduring. Shrubs love to grow, some big and strong, others tall and lanky, and some have very sharp, prickly fingers. Shrubs teach us about humility in that we don't really need to protect ourselves from outside sources, we just need to be who we are and exude our energy in any way we choose. No harm can really come to us if we are truly experiencing our real nature. We, as spiritual beings, can learn to be trusted in what we do based upon what we put out into our energy field. Shrubs are pretty much forthright and that is what shrub beings want to explain to us. They do enjoy engagement with others, particularly humans, and that engagement might be one of a physical kind (falling into a prickly bush) or of the esoteric kind (offering their energy to recharge our doubts and fears into non-existence). Shrubs are clean and pure in their energy source and they can offer you a well of information about fear, greed, protective sources, and worries. They are experts in clearing energy patterns that no longer serve and they can offer clear thoughts on why your behavior isn't working for you anymore. This is the predominant offerings that shrubs have for our human experience.

A beautiful green hedge presented itself to me and offered me these words of wisdom and advice:

"We offer clear guidance on how to let go of that which dominates your thoughts and worries. We can provide you with insight into clearing your thoughts and fears and doubts from your mind and heart and allow your true nature to come spilling through. Clarity is ease of mind and will allow you to be more of your true nature in all that you do. Fear must not be allowed to dictate what you choose to do. Fear is a mechanism for knowing your true self, yet most of you get absorbed in becoming your fears rather than alleviating them. Fear can be consuming and detrimental, if you do not allow it to be consumed by truth."

◆ ◆ ✿ ◆ ◆

Bread feeds the body, indeed, but flowers feed also the soul.

- The Quran

FLOWERS

Flower beings are about light and enjoying the energy of life all around. Flowers bring forth life and require light to function and create more. Flower beings love beauty and although their lives tend to be short, mostly, all flower beings want to experience life as renewal. Flowers work towards creating energy and sustaining their existence through mutual givings. They give and receive simultaneously and they want to encourage others to do the same. They are experts in creating and handling balance, and plant and flower beings work synonymously to create an experience previously uncreated. They work harmoniously to bring new life and great joy through their creations and flower beings love to spread their life to other places, energetically and physically.

Flowers are balanced givers and makers as they create their lives. They receive from the air and light above and take what they need or want from the ground below and in return, they give beauty, grace, elegance, and perpetuation of the next generation. They can help balance your life and your energy just simply by inviting them into your life. Cut flowers are an easy way to achieve this balance, as long as you ask the flower beings permission to remove them from their previous physical location. This offers respect and honors their achievements and they in turn will give you much more life than if you just remove them by force. If a flower grouping has already been cut (i.e. you bought them in a store or market or someone gave them to you), then honor and acknowledge the flower beings for their work and creation and they will give you extra offerings throughout their duration. Flower beings love to give, they just ask to be honored first.

Not all flowers offer the same kind of message or offerings. Some will give extra brightness, some beauty, some words or advice, others fresher air and cleaning your space.

"Flowers are beings of joy and gratitude. Flowers love to create and maintain beauty within themselves and their outward expression. Flowers come in all shapes and sizes, colors and patterns. This allows for new creativity at each avenue of creation. Around every corner of new life, there is something new to be experienced, something odd to be loved, and something bold to be cherished. We love to create in lots and lots of ways and we will share our techniques of creation with you if you allow us to shine into your lives. We provide hope and understanding, light and love, joy and gratitude. Our lives are wondrous creations of new enchantment and every spring we endure to return. We radiate new life, new love, new everything because in the newness, there is

pleasure, excitement, joy, and renewal. This we can offer to you in the form of our message of this life we lead. Come join us in joy!"

Flowers are very easy beings to communicate with and they love to share their wisdom and insight into their colorful creations. Enjoy their experience!

Those who labour in the earth are the chosen people of God.
- Thomas Jefferson

Every message from grass, plant, shrub and flower beings will be different and specific to the area you are asking about or what you are currently experiencing. It is not important to know what type of nature being they are or even what physical specimen they are, unless that is of interest to you. What is important is the message they provide, the connection to the earth and air they offer, and their amazing Divine nature. Keep plants in your home, as they will enliven the area you live in and clean the energetic space. If you are unsure based upon how much "work" they might be, go to the store or nursery where you will be purchasing them and ask them. Feel to see if they are the right match for your personality and theirs.

Flowers and plants of all kinds are Divine beings seeking to provide you insight into your own life of creation. They will inspire you and show you how to make new changes of happiness, prosperity, resourcefulness, and ingenuity in maintaining a new life of love and joy. Use your plants, grass, shrubs and flowers to work new lines of creation and allow them to invite positive hope into your life of new life.

To speak truly, few adult persons can see nature. Most persons do not see the sun. At least they have a very superficial seeing. The sun illuminates only the eye of the man, but shines into the eye and heart of the child. The lover of nature is he whose inward and outward senses are still truly adjusted to each other; who has retained the spirit of infancy even into the era of manhood.

- Ralph Waldo Emerson

We need to find God, and he cannot be found in noise and restlessness. God is the friend of silence. See how nature - trees, flowers, grass - grows in silence; see the stars, the moon and the sun, how they move in silence... We need silence to be able to touch souls.

- Mother Teresa

Three things cannot be long hidden:
the Sun, the Moon and the Truth.

- Buddha

THE SUN, THE MOON, AND FIRE

♦ ♦ ✿ ♦ ♦

After all this time, the sun never says to the earth, you
owe me. Look what happens with a love like that. It lights
up the whole sky.

– Hafiz, 13ᵗʰ century
Sufi poet

SUNBEAM BEINGS

On a recent trip to Arizona, a friend and I rented a convertible to cruise around in. Not only was it fun to drive, but we knew it'd be that much easier to access all the various beings as we whipped around the countryside. Of course, in a convertible, our concern drew towards getting sunburned and in today's world, there is a mass market sunscreen and sunblock campaign against skin cancer. On this trip, I knew I wanted to communicate with the sunbeam beings, which of course you can do from anywhere, but with such strong continual media influence, my thoughts still turned toward the fear of getting sunburned.

As we drove with the top down, I had a strong urging to not put anything on my skin. Since my friend was driving, I was able to sit quietly with my energy and ask the sunbeam beings how to not get sunburned and why we do get sunburned. This is what they had to say about sunburns, sunblock, and redness and heat in our skin:

"Your skin becomes enflamed because you've trapped us and you resist us. We are not here to harm you or your bodies. Your bodies need us. We are not unlike the sun that comes through your windowpanes. The windowpanes do not burn, but the energy just flows right through. We can flow right through you too, but there is much resistance about us in your world. You fear us and what we do, therefore we cannot provide you with what you desire. The sunblock you place on your skin just reinforces your resistance and loathing for us. We just want to nurture you and pass through you like a windowpane allowing warmth, nutrition, and ease. We dance on your skin when you push back at us rather than let us flow through you. We will not hurt you, nor will we burn you if you come to work with us. We are always here to help you, warm you and nourish you. Allow us through. You are our windowpane.

"Skin cancer is about loathing us to your core and fear of being nourished. We do not despise you, nor do we wish for you to despise us. We want to work in harmony for each of us has our purpose in this plane. Allow us in and we will work with you. It may take some time as many of you have sought alternatives for too much time and your thoughts are clouded about us, but we will work with you. Talk to us, for we are always here. Harnessing the energy of the sun is our mission and giving life to living things with this energy is our job. Use us as a means for warmth and light and

we will repay you with kindness and gentleness. *Embrace us in your daily living for we come to heal the earth in its purest form. We are healers, not destroyers unlike what we have been described.*

"We are like the fire beings and yet we are different; some similarities, some differences. We wish for peace and warmth in your bodies and in your souls because peace and warmth in your body and soul will bring peace and warmth to our planet. We wish for a divine planet stage where wind, fire, water, earth and space all work as one. One. We are achieving this goal, but you, as much as we, are all five elements and you must gain control of your choices. We are very passionate beings of the sun. There are many suns, but yours is only one and this one we have chosen to speak through as a means to communicate our goals. We seek peace and harmony in the celestial realm, which encompasses the earthly realm. Please know that every choice you make is one that distributes evenly among all of us, all beings, and one of peace and warmth will bring greater understanding to you all about our world in the nonphysical realm. You gain truth by working with us and asking us for guidance, for our purpose is to warm your soul. Our physical abilities are merely for pleasure or pain, a physical reaction, but our ultimate goal is peace and love-warmth. This we can achieve together. Please come to us, as so few do in your realm, and we will instill peace among you-living."

During the time I communicated with them and worked with them, my skin did not get hot, red or burned for almost two hours of driving mid-day in 100 degree weather while my friend's turned bright red. I told her about my conversation with the sunbeam beings and she immediately began to practice the windowpane suggestion. After several more hours of driving and as our thoughts drifted to other things, my skin began to turn a little pink and my friend's was still red, so we asked the sunbeam beings and our guides for clarification. My friend and I were both told that just as when we were babies and learning to walk, some things take practice until they become second-nature. Just as walking has become an unconscious effort (most of the time!), so will our exchange with the sunbeam beings as we turn off old thought forms about skin cancer and sun protection and allow new ones of loving warmth, nutrient absorption, and blessed light to permeate our existence. We are both happy to say we practiced and communicated with the sunbeam beings during our entire trip and after a week with the top down and the sunbeams passing through us, we received very little skin color change and only gave into old sunscreen patterns on a couple of days when we knew we could not hold our connection for extended periods of time. Listen to your guidance as you change your thought patterns, if they need changing at all, and ask the sunbeam beings for insight and guidance about working with them. And remember that just as they are energy, so are we, for energy is all there is and once you begin to see that everything is energy and nothing is not, then we can pass the sunbeams through us, garner their nutritional value, warmth and light, and allow the rest to pass right through us like a windowpane.

Everyone is a moon, and has a dark side which he never shows to anybody.

- Mark Twain

MOONBEAM BEINGS

Moonbeam beings look much like their physical counterparts with white shimmery bodies that flow and move as light and air. Moonbeams can be elusive to people wanting to communicate with them because they do not spend as much time with people on a waking basis as do other beings like the sunbeam beings. When the moonbeam beings come to visit, they tend to share their information through energy exchange and use of healing techniques and tools. The moonbeams are healers in many different ways and they offer us significant insight into our world, as well as theirs, if only we ask. The key is we must go to them. Unlike sunbeams who talk to us all the time, moonbeams prefer to do their work quietly and off the radar, so to speak. They guide people and show the way to cleaner living through waste reduction and management of recyclables (energy). Guiding others is their primary chore and offering tools and techniques of healing is secondary. Most beings who live on this planet have their own agenda of experiencing, yet the moonbeams have a much less self-propelled motive to being here. Moonbeams come from many places, in terms of their origin of being, and they are truly considered star beings. Rituals performed under the light of the moon always involve the moonbeams and they are eager to help in healing and cleansing people, places, and things. Call upon the moonbeam beings for assistance with clearing, clarity, determination, and elimination of all things unnatural or unhelpful in your life. These beings are truly helper beings with a clear agenda for assistance.

When I first met a moonbeam being, I had already spent quite some time talking and working with countless other types of beings. I had wanted to communicate with the moonbeams, yet they seemed quite elusive until finally one night as I drove home from a friend's house, there was a beautiful crescent moon in the sky and for the first time a beautiful moonbeam being was visible. At the time, I was only able to connect with one moonbeam being until I began writing this section. As soon as I began to realize what great helpers and healers they are, yet elusive until you ask for their help, then could I begin to see more and more of them. Seeing and experiencing the moonbeams takes a little more effort and patience, but the outcome is well worth the wait. Also keep in mind that once you connect with the moonbeam beings, they will visit you anytime, anywhere, if you are in need of assistance or just want to be with them. It just may take some time for them to present themselves, but always know that they are there.

The next day, as I sat in my garden, another moonbeam friend came to visit. I invited the moonbeam to sit next to me on my swing and the being touched my arm gently without ever saying a word. When my mind began to wander elsewhere, the moonbeam being stopped what it was doing and began to leave. I quickly asked my friend to stay and learned that in order to experience the moonbeams, you must stay engaged in the exchange. They are healers, but if the one they have come to work with is not in a place to receive, they will kindly choose to leave and return later. My friend returned to a seated position and resumed the energy exchange which felt quite subtle, yet even as I write this several hours later, I can still feel the exchange on my arm where the being touched me. The feeling is light and gentle and subtle just as moon energy can be, however it is also long-lasting and tremendously powerful. I had not called upon the moonbeams for a particular healing, but I trust them and their wisdom to know what is necessary for the type of healing they offer. After the exchange, my moonbeam friend had this to say:

"Brethren, you have asked for our assistance for millennia or longer in earth times. We welcome your requests as they build a network of allies between our world and yours. We are here to help you as many more are to come. We offer you light and hope

and love and peaceful joy in your lives. We do come to those who request our help and we are present at moonlight ceremonies and rituals to assist in energy exchanges. Our goal is to assist and cure those who ail in fight; to assist those who seek not false hope; and to aid those who have fallen into falsehoods. We gather information and store it in the stars for those who seek greater allied information. We introduce partnerships between many worldly beings as a new exchange of ideas, information and technology. We offer hope in places of despair among those who cannot see the light in the daytime. We come quietly to places and dwellings where hope has been lost and it can be restored upon asking. Call to us for gathering information. Call to us for help in your heart, home and for hope. Call to us for weather and purpose in being. We come for rescue in the stars of old for we are always here and ready when you are ready to receive hope again. We are not elusive; we choose specifically. We come to all who call us and show ourselves to those who seek us and we are always there. For those who do not see us, know that we are still there. We ask forgiveness where forgiveness has been stolen. We offer peace and hope in places where hope has been forgotten. We offer relief in times of great need across this great world. We dispel myths of gods who seek not to help, but rather harm. We offer wisdom in exchange for loyalty in knowing us. We provide moonlight to show others their way. This is why we have come and why we come to the few who ask us. The information and experience must be sought. We are always here to help you. Always. Ask for us anytime you need our help and we will be there helping you in many, many ways. Thank you for allowing our light to shine.”

Each separate dying ember wrought its ghost upon the floor.
- Edgar Allan Poe

FIRE

Fire beings are powerful magnets of energy and enthusiasm for change and assistance to our needs. We have the power to call fire to help us create and rejuvenate, instead of destroy or manipulate. Fire traditionally has been used to procure disease, manifest destinies, tell fortunes and speak to the afterworld. Fire beings do not destroy that which has not been asked of them. They do not see destruction and creation as separate entities. To them, they are the same. It is about building and creating desires and wishes from nothingness. Destruction is just simply another means of achieving the same outcome.

Fire beings are generally red, yellow, orange or blue in auric color and they present themselves harshly. They are not benevolent or malevolent beings, as this does not matter to them. What they do want is to create and manifest greater realities with their constituents, those who seek their assistance. Fire beings will come and give you energy surges, bolder feelings and stronger thoughts. They will allow you to manifest and create based on what you truly ask for and they will do it quickly, efficiently, and without remorse, so be careful what you ask for. They are very powerful beings and they are also great healers. Truth be told, no one can heal another without their consent for change and the same holds true for the fire beings. They, however, have the ability to manifest deep, lasting change that will literally ignite you to move forward and strive for more. Fire beings provide warmth, security, petulance, and resistance to outward or inward deviance – that is, going against your soul's highest truth. These beings will work with any who ask for their assistance to connect to their own highest truths or for those who need a spark of inspiration. Fire burns inside all of us and many times, depression is a result of a lost spark which fire can help you regain. Anger can be a sign of fire assistance, and if it is used for creating instead of destroying, it can reunite you with the love of yourself and your fondest dreams.

Fire beings will come to you if you need their assistance, if you ask them. Sometimes you may not know they are there, yet they will show up in colorful ways. Signs of fire can be anger, frustration, growth, movement, inspired thoughts or ideas, joy, love, and so much more. If you are working with fire, you will know it.

One day, I sat on my deck swinging in my bench swing and enjoying my backyard full of nature beings, when I noticed a very brilliant red-orange being standing with another being I had not experienced before. I invited the nature beings to join me and the fire being expressed urgency that there was a message for me to write. He continued to urge and nudge me to move and up to my computer I went to share this message:

"We want all those to know that we are here to serve, not to be frightened of. We want a connection with you and your sources. We want to work with you to solve problems related to fire and storms. We have much heat about being who we are and who you are. We are passionate and compassionate, but we can only serve those who ask us for our help. We tire of the blame and fear associated with our existence, for this is not who we are. We are servers. We are helpers. We are grantors. We are mechanics of light and beingness. We serve a greater purpose of propulsion of light, beingness and creation of all living things by spark and fire. We can serve by those willing to allow us to come and help you. Call us for help with igniting flame in your plants, animals and people. We inspire, provoke, instigate and design new techniques for passion, pleasure, and teaching. Ask us for help to create a new life. Ask us to fire up your inner most being. Ask us to participate in creating a better dwelling. Ask us to flame the love in your life. We call upon those who seek greater universal truth by knowing that all elements can create as easily as they can destroy, so call upon those who offer change, hope, and eternal lasting creation.

"Yes, of course, there are fire beings who wish to destroy. Do not call upon them for assistance in your life unless that is

what you wish to experience. Call upon us, those who wish to create a better life and world through fiery flames of desire, creation and institution. We seek you as you seek help. We are always there to assist you, just call. Why do those of you who wish for change not call? Call us daily, momentarily, infinitely. We wish to assist you in your changes. But be prepared for the outcome. You may not always like what we garner for you, yet trust it is for your highest good. For we see the passion inside you unfolding and unfurling like a newly born leaf, only you need a spark of desire, creation, instigating. That we can provide. Call upon us who breathe fire to provide that for you and we shall provide. Just be prepared to accept the inflow of greatness that we shall set free. Just as a forest may burn in a fire, there is new, more powerful growth created by that change. There are no accidents, no victims, no tragedy. Only what is called upon and called forth.

"Know that we will never harm you, for we are here to help if that is what you wish. We may create and begin the causing of change that seems unnecessary for you. Rest assured, it is. And we hold your highest in regard. Fire is the means of being alive, as are all elements you inhabit in your body. Fire, water, earth, air. All these things you must have to survive in your physicalness. Let fire create your desire, your yearning for more in this world. Let fire be your next step in change. Call upon us frequently and change will happen rapidly. We will make the way. We will make your way. Call for us."

Five key words for working with Fire Beings:

- *Change*
- *Creativity*
- *Spark*
- *Life*
- *Evolution*

Fire beings are an excellent example of nature beings who desire to help and assist us in many ways. They can help us create, they can inspire us, they can help us manifest, or they can help us destroy. We can work with them to create our lives as we wish and desire or we can use them to hurt ourselves and destroy that which is all around us. Even in destruction of a great forest by a fire, there is new life born out of the ashes. Some plants can only thrive and survive on the ashes of lava, and fire can create the life of the plant that must grow there. There is always creation; it is just a matter of the evolution of the process and the reaction of the onlookers as to which process it is. That is the only distinction.

Fire beings are distinct beings who procreate their lives with the power of the ethereal realm. The fire beings work to protect and procure powerful forces of change and provocation within themselves, as well as in others who seek their assistance. Fire beings are available without the use of fire itself, as fire is a powerful force within all entities, all beings, all of nature. You can experience fire without the physical experience of fire manifesting before you. Simply allow it to manifest within you and seek the answers there.

When working with fire, be forewarned that fire beings are highly charged, electrical entities that will give the feeling of force in your life. Fire beings, like all nature beings, will never force you to change or exude new behaviors. Instead, they will allow you and encourage you to bring forth new opportunities, new changes and new desires through highly active means. By inviting fire as a non-physical entity into your life, you invoke and reignite powerful changes and powerful manifestation abilities into your core. These beings are excited to work with you and they will provide new avenues of change and creation in ways only previously dreamed.

Remember this. When people choose to withdraw far from a fire, the fire continues to give warmth, but they grow cold. When people choose to withdraw far from light, the light continues to be bright in itself, but they are in darkness. This is also the case when people withdraw from God.

– Augustine

Look deep into nature, and then you will understand everything better.

- Albert Einstein

EPILOGUE

If we could see the miracle of a single flower clearly, our whole life would change.

- Buddha

From understanding comes awareness, which belates hostility and motivates calmness and consideration among all beings. Once we begin to know what and who we really are and what and who is really around us, there can be no fear, for all is exposed and understood. This can take time, patience, and practice, so be gentle with yourself and trust what you know, what you hear, what you feel, and what you are. For this will ultimately allow you to become greater and more aware of the truth of all universes. This Universe is one that allows us a chance to unfold in our own space-time and create ourselves over and over and over again. By gaining perspective on how this works within our world, we can allow ourselves to become more knowledgeable, better understood, and grow to greater lengths than we have ever grown before. This is our purpose here. This is why we came. We came to experience ourselves, our surroundings, and what is possible for us to create from the truth within us. Nature can allow us a glimpse into a world where creation happens quickly, efficiently, mindlessly, and without hesitation. There is no fear because no matter what is created, all is beautiful and a masterpiece. And if the creator does not care for the creation, then simply create again. That is the process. Try new things, try new avenues, and above all, give it all you've got - no matter what it is. This will result in long-term happiness, untold personal power and satisfaction, and great achievements.

A bird does not sing because it has an answer. It sings because it has a song.

- Chinese Proverb

Nature beings are a quick link to Earth and Earth's centeredness, and in relation to achieving our own goals, the nature beings can help us achieve our greatest wishes by observing their abilities, asking for their wisdom and assistance, and navigating our Earthly ethereal plane with great skill and charisma. Chasms in the Earth's energy prevent us from recognizing one another with the frequency and vibration that nature beings experience one another, but we can overcome this obstacle that we have created with disbelief and disarmament of spirit. We can overcome this challenge by allowing them back into our lives, welcoming their presence and assuring them that we do not intend to use them or their information for harm and deceit. They are acutely aware of this information prior to our experiences with them, yet they want to know if we know it consciously and whether we are truly aware of our own intentions towards them. The nature beings will provide us with insight and awareness, but predominantly those who seek to work with us do so with unabashed charm and grace and they do not wish to condone disillusionment or energy that is counterproductive to their own needs here on Earth. They are sensitive to this and much more developed in reading someone's true intention and if this is the case, then you will not see them or experience their greatness. Allowing them into your life to assist you with knowing and assist them in gaining greater understanding of humankind from an individual perspective will foster global and universal connections and unlimited potential for understanding our worlds beyond physical realities. This is key for their desire to connect with us, and if they connect to that within you, the communication will be easy, unguarded, and flowing like water. Communication with all spirits of nature is an old tradition, and centuries ago, mankind did it with ease, grace and without contemplation. Now, we must take a little effort combined with patience and the ability to listen and wait for them to connect to us, in order for us to regain our previously easy channel.

The best remedy for those who are afraid, lonely or unhappy is to go outside, somewhere where they can be quiet, alone with the heavens, nature and God. Because only then does one feel that all is as it should be and that God wishes to see people happy, amidst the simple beauty of nature.

- Anne Frank

The nature beings are plentiful and waiting to connect with anyone looking for honest awareness and greater understanding of their world, their lives, and their stories. The trees, rocks, clouds, flowers, and waters of the world await a deep, enjoyable, lasting connection with the spiritual beings of humankind and they want to share their experiences with you. They want to know you and your existence and assist you with solutions for problems they themselves have overcome. Nature beings are exact in their proposals to humans and they will enlist your help in return for their assistance. Their requests tend to be in uplifting nature, giving energetic assistance or physical assistance by cleaning up an area or feeding an area's spirit with physical or spiritual infusions. They will let you know what they expect in return, if anything at all. Some beings want to just offer assistance or experience human interaction. Others want to work with you and uplift and inspire you as you do the same for them. They need and want us as much as we need and want them as we are all interconnected and each interlocking piece makes a complete puzzle. You just have to know that you are a puzzle piece and find where you fit.

Those who dwell among the beauties and mysteries of the earth are never alone or weary of life.

- Rachel Carson

Nature beings preserve their energies for creation and manifestation of all kinds and they are masters at energetic abilities. Many of us wish for more power and knowledge in our lives, rather than force and struggle through inability and lack of confidence. The nature beings will assist and show you how to maintain a new sense of identity that includes all spectrums of the self and the Oneness, not just the individual meanderings. New truths will be formed simply by engaging with nature and all the aspects of nature. New thoughts will foster new creations and inspired ideas for manifestation that previously did not exist simply by connecting with nature. Whole formations of energetic masterpieces will be thrust forward as if divinely inspired simply by working with the beings of nature and allowing them in. Nature beings are complex in their varied multitudes, yet simplistic in their desires, ability to create and know, and their absolute connectedness to Earth and the source of all things. This alone will inspire you to move forward captivatingly into their world, which is above all things, *our world*. The nature beings exist in all places, in all times, in all moments, in all things and they create and maintain the beauty that is our planet. Their global universalness is unlimited and unyielding and they can show you the option of making a beautiful life too. This is their wish for us, to truly know what we are and what we are capable of as spiritual beings of all that is. In essence, in the core, we are exactly that which is the makings of a nature being, only our chosen experiences make us different. This understanding, this connection will allow us to move into a place where great things happen and wondrous worlds occur. This is what nature really is and why they want to talk to you. They are eager to show you more of your true self, the self that is all things, in all places, in all moments, in all times. And they want to show you the beauty that is your true nature.

Forests, lakes, and rivers, clouds and winds, stars and flowers, stupendous glaciers and crystal snowflakes – every form of animate or inanimate existence, leaves its impress upon the soul of man.

- Orison Swett Marden

FREQUENTLY ASKED QUESTIONS ABOUT NATURE BEINGS

Frequently, I am asked questions about what I do and about the many types of entities in which I encounter. How do you know if it's real? How do you know what you are really seeing? What kinds of things will I experience? These will be different for every person, but there are some things I have learned along the way that may help you in your own adventures. Here is a list of some of the more popular FAQs I have been asked and that you may be asked one day too.

The power to question is the basis of all human progress.
- Indira Gandhi

Q: *How do I know what I see (feel, hear, or just know) is real?*

If you see it, hear it, feel it, or just know it, it's real. No one can tell you what is real for you or for someone else, and truth be told, what is real is a matter of perspective. Reality comes from an individual point of view and it is up to the individual to decide what they want to be real for them and true for their existence. I cannot tell you what is true and what is not, only that I know for myself and for the nature beings, their existence is very real in that all spiritual beings have an existence. There are many points of philosophy that argue that all physical existence is an illusion. This is true in that all physical existence is no more real than the creation that it is created to be. There is a difference between an illusion and a hallucination. A hallucination is something that we make up out of fear or desire. An illusion is something that exists, but we make it more real than it truly is. We stop seeing it for what and how it really exists. All energy that runs through all things is equally the same and we all have it, no matter what we are. Energy is just energy, it just depends on how dense or free it is and in what state it exists for however long it chooses to exist that way. Life is free flowing and moving constantly and what we choose to be real for our experience will ebb and flow as much as the tides do. Choosing what is real for you is an individual choice, but if you know in your heart and you believe in your being that what you see is true, then it is. For you. What matters most is what you do with your chosen beliefs and how you choose to express them or react to them. Trusting your guidance to show you what is real and applicable for you is all it takes to have clairvoyance, clairaudience, clairsentience, or claircognizance. But these are just labels. The truth is, you will see and experience the world however you want to experience it. You can see it as full and overflowing, half-full, half-empty, or not even there at all. That is up to you. But, I can tell you that what exists out there is much more far reaching than our physical eye will ever lead us to believe. It's all a matter of choosing to remember.

Q: *I am not seeing or experiencing anything. Am I doing something wrong?*

You cannot experience it incorrectly. There are some who are more adept at perceiving information than others, yet all it takes is a little practice, effort, patience, and persistence. You can achieve all that you wish to achieve, if you believe in yourself and what is possible for you. Don't give up. Keep trying if you feel what you are doing will pay off for you in the end. If not, try something new. There are many, many avenues to receiving guidance and information from the universe and each of us does so in our own unique way. Trust what you get and don't slap it down as minute or unimportant. All information received is important, no matter how trivial one might believe it to be. Start with what you have and what you are getting now, even if that appears to be nothing, trust your instincts and keep moving forward. Ask your guides, your Angels, and the nature beings for more information and thank the Universe for sending it to you in a way that you can receive it best. When I first relearned to open myself to communication, I kept asking the Universe to send it to me clearly, concisely, and in the easiest, most blatant way possible. And they did. Trust yourself. It will come.

Q: *If they are like us, why don't rocks and trees move?*

They do move. Plants move, trees move, rocks move. Just because they don't move like we move – fast, quick and hurried most of the time – doesn't mean they don't move. There has been recorded research shown that a tree or plant will move itself to a better location, if it needs to or wants to. Many times, trees and rocks will enjoy the location it chose to experience initially and never choose to move. Others move repeatedly. Human beings are exactly the same way. They sometimes choose to move far from their original home location to explore and endure new experiences and others will live right across the street from where they grew up. It's about choice and desire. Not all choices and desires will be the same.

Trees, rocks, and other nature beings move in a different space-time than humans do. Light speed is faster than most humans move and yet we know that light moves. To the light, we would look like we were moving at slower than snail speed; potentially it could even look like we are not moving at all even though in our space-time experience, we can see clearly that each of us is moving. Each aspect of nature lives in a different space-time. And that space-time will dictate how another aspect of nature perceives the movements of one another. So, really it is just a matter of perspective.

Q: *Aren't you just anthropomorphizing or personifying nature into human form?*

The truth is, we all see and experience exactly what we want to experience. We can choose to block out or ignore what is around us all the time, in all things, or we can choose to embrace them and allow them to teach us more about their truths and their existence. The nature beings will look like what is easiest for us to recognize as something other than our physical self. If that being comes through in the outline of a person, then so be it. If that aspect of nature shows itself in the form of an ethereal abstract, so be it. However it will make sense to us and will be recognizable as the entity and the energy that is trying to connect to us, that is what we will experience.

Each of us experiences everything in a uniquely different way. No two people experience the same moment in exactly the same way, but when those two people reminisce about it, they intrinsically know it to be the same moment by what they have experienced and what they remember about that moment. However, they each have a unique perspective on that moment and what was experienced in that moment. It is even possible for those two people to remember completely different things about that moment, as though they were living a different experience in the same moment. The same is true for connecting to nature beings. If we choose not to experience non-physical beings in any particular form (or ask for the experience in any particular format) then we will hear, feel, see, or just know that they exist, which is truly their most original form, as is our true, original form. The soul does not occupy a particular interest in any one form. It morphs to provide the illusion that will allow it to convey the message most accurately and with the best reception. That is how nature beings work and exist at their core, and it is true for all forms of energy and spirit.

Q: *I am seeing and experiencing something different than what you describe. Why is that?*

Each of us will experience a different type of experience. Just as you are having a life that is completely your own and no one will fully experience it the same way you do, even if they were living the exact same life, this is true for how we perceive things. Not all of us perceive and assimilate the world in the exact same way. Some will see, some will hear, some feel, and others just know. Beyond how you take in information, there is the difference in how things will present themselves to you. Each of us could be looking at the exact same piece of art, but will we all see the same thing? We might see the same basic ideas about that piece of art, but each of us will experience it in a different way and whatever works for you is perfect for you. Don't discount something because your friend didn't see it exactly the same way you did or vice versa.

A friend and I like to meditate and travel together to experience new parts of creation. When we are experiencing those, we have noticed that many times she sees things a certain way and I see them another, yet we see the same basic things. It is a matter of perspective and how she sees and experiences the world and how I see and experience the world. It is fun for us to compare notes and look at the event from different points of view, hers and mine. This is true for all experiences. Try to think of a memory that involved two or more people, including yourself. Now, go and find those people and discuss the details of that memory. For the most part, each of you will remember different things and see it from your individual, unique perspective. It doesn't mean one is right and another is wrong; it just means you have a unique perspective on the world. Seeing things differently allows us to broaden our perspective universally. If we experienced everything exactly the same as each other all the time, then there would be no need to be individual or unique. We could just stay as homogeneous God-consciousness and absorb the information from each other. There is no creation in that, only absorption and boredom. As spiritual beings, part of our desire to be individual was to have a unique perspective, an individual experience. It doesn't mean we are less than the whole or separate; it just means we have an optional point of view to share with all spiritual beings.

Q: *Will my friends and I always experience different things or will we be able to experience the same things?*

You can experience the same things. This is always possible. As was answered previously, part of our desire to be individual was to have a unique perspective to share with all spiritual beings. This unique perspective can be shared with another individual or a group and it can be done clearly, concisely, and effectively if all parties are in agreement as to whose viewpoint is being experienced. This can allow for a homogeneous experience, but some work must be done to achieve this. Not all people are capable of it because most of us are deeply involved in our individual experience. Non-physical entities who have worked to achieve this and have agreed upon this type of experience have been able to achieve homogeneity. Of course, you don't have to be in non-physical form or homogeneous to experience a similar experience. It just takes practice, patience, and strong communication between the various parties to allow for a unified, singular perspective experience. If this is what you wish, then I say go for it, but don't discount the valuable experience of multiple points of view and seeing things from many different perspectives. This can be much more fulfilling and a richer experience because not only do you experience your own experience, you now experience many others from their colorful point of view. You get to experience them as an individual and the event from several different points of view. This can allow for a broadening and an expansion. Neither is better, they are just simply different and it is up to the individual to choose their experience either way.

Q: *Why do you choose to call them nature beings instead of devas, fairies, or what others have been told to call them before?*

All nature beings have had communication with human beings since the dawn of time. Since there was nature, there have been nature beings and if you only knew how many beings there were everywhere, all the time, you could then understand why so many names exist for different types of entities. Calling them nature beings simplifies them and prevents them from falling into a label and a categorization, for the most part. Yes, there are devas, menehunes, wood sprites, fairies, gnomes, leprechauns, etc. and each of these beings have their own experiences, their own creations, and their own manifestations to behold. The nature beings I describe are the beings who inhabit or oversee specific aspects of nature. Elementals, such as those described above, have an important role in nature, and yet they are different (most of them) than the nature beings I have chosen to write about. Think of a corporation. Inside that corporation, there are lots of jobs, lots of people, lots of things to do, create, maintain, oversee, and regulate. All aspects of existence are like this, only on a much, much, much larger scale. There are beings for literally everything. This book describes only a very, very, very small portion of spiritual beings out there having a physical or non-physical experience. With each type of spiritual being expressed and experienced, there is a new chance for communication, a new chance for understanding, and a new opportunity to see the world as it really exists in its infinite vastness. I suggest you take an opportunity to really experience nature and all the beings who inhabit, create and maintain the physical experiences we call nature. Experience them and decide for yourself. That truly is the best route to understanding.

Q: *Can a nature being choose to leave its physical inhabitance? Can an aspect of nature exist without a nature being?*

Nature beings typically stay with their physical existence until the physical existence no longer exists in its current physical form. Many times the beings will continue on and create a new physical existence from the old previous physical incarnation or sometimes it will move on and find a new home. The latter behavior is more typical of cloud, wind, and transient nature beings. Those nature beings more closely related to the earth (trees, plants, flowers) tend to create a new physical existence after the de-construction of the prior existence.

Nature beings tend to stay with their creation and see it through the end. There are few exceptions and rarities where nature beings become entrapped in their existence and need help getting out. There are other nature beings, elementals, and spiritual assistants who help with these situations. Nature rarely just leaves a physical existence without greater awareness, just as your soul would not just leave your body haphazardly. There are always rare exceptions to any rule and there are cases where instances have happened both in nature and in humans.

A physical entity cannot exist without something or someone to create its existence. The nature being does not have to inhabit its physical creation, it can simply watch and observe as things manifest, but a creation needs to have a creator. If one creator leaves, another will enter. This is part of those rare circumstances. Without the energy that is needed to hold a creation in form, which comes from the creator, the creation ceases to exist. The energy does not dissipate, it simply changes form. All energy is fluid and in motion at all times. It is just a matter of density that maintains a form. From this density comes many varied creations of wondrous proportions and this includes souls, both human and nature in origin. Just as there are creators for physical manifestations, there are creators for non-physical manifestations, and they too must be overseen.

Everybody needs beauty as well as bread, places to play in and pray in, where nature may heal and give strength to body and soul.

- John Muir

A SPECIAL MESSAGE
FROM THE JELLYFISH

Jellies (as they are known in the marine world) are obviously physical entities, but their message to us is inherently non-physical. I have encountered and communicated with many physical animals, as well as non-physical animals, and the message I received from the jellies stood out so profoundly that I felt compelled to include a special section dedicated to them.

But ask the animals, and they will teach you;
the birds of the air, and they will tell you;
ask the plants of the earth, and they will teach you;
and the fish of the sea will declare to you.
- Job 12:7-8

On a recent trip to Shark Reef in Las Vegas, of all places, I found myself mesmerized while watching this monumental cylindrical water tank that held about 100 moon jellies. The aquarium was very busy and packed with people, particularly this area because there is a one-finger-touching exhibit in the same room. Even while the people paraded by, I was instantly drawn to the beauty of this tank. The jellies cascaded up and down the sides of their tank simply, easily, and with little effort. I found myself pressed against the glass with my hands up on the tank and my head and chest pressed into the glass. Of course, I do not recommend tapping on the glass as this can be quite disturbing to the animals inside, but in this case, I found myself suctioned up to them, sans the tapping. I could feel the energy pulsating inside, not like electricity, but more like a wave of energy. As I was pressed to the glass, I cleared my mind ready to receive a message if one should come and instead I found that the jellies were attracted to me and began to cascade down my front side and down by where my hands were. As they passed by each of my chakras, a strong opening and cleansing sensation occurred. I began to realize they were cleaning me and my energy! I asked the friend I was with to do the same and see what happens. She did and the jellies began to migrate down her chakras and through her hands and she reported the same feeling. I noticed that any children nearby who had their hands pressed to the glass were also receiving the same benefits. I was fascinated and completely intrigued by this incredible experience and I just stayed poised against the glass, mind clear, body receiving. Eventually, several of the biggest of the jellies came down through my centers with the strongest, most powerful energy sweep and I began to hear their message to me:

"*Peace.*

    Peace.

       Heal.

We are the healers of the sea.

We are here to heal the sea and all its creatures.

Peace and harmony prevail wherever we are found.

We as One bring peace to the sea and all its inhabitants.

Peace and harmony.
We heal the sea."

Their words were few, but the peaceful energy that came from them was highly intense. The jellies had the most amazing effect on me. In an extremely chaotic and highly crowded room, I felt completely at peace with a stillness in my body and in my mind. I was absolutely amazed at the effect their cleansing had on me. Because I am empathic, and as most empathics are, I tend to become overstimulated in crowded places because of all the energy flowing through me and around me so rapidly. For once, this was absolutely not the case! Even my friend recognized the difference in my energy. They had given me an amazing amount of cleansing and clarity.

If you have a mission of peace and healing on this planet, I highly recommend you go visit jellies, either in the ocean or in a well-loved and well-tended aquarium. Please be respectful by not tapping on the glass or touching them in the water as their bodies are quite delicate, but just engage with them energetically and telepathically and you will absolutely be amazed.

After my experience with the moon jellies, I spent some time at the beach near my home and as I walked along, I found a colony of fried egg jellies (they are clear with a yellow center, so they look like a raw or a fried egg) and one jelly followed me down the beach. I spoke with it and realized the message was just as clear that day as the day at the aquarium with the same implied meaning. In the simplicity of their physical being, they have come with a very profound message for peace and healing. They choose a life of grace to promote an energy so many of us desire, but have forgotten how to exude. Don't forget to thank the jellies for the work they are doing here for the benefit of all of us when you take time to visit the energy and animals of the sea. You might be amazed at the connection you receive and the energy you can then put forth into so many other places. It is a gift that will keep on giving.

Acknowledgements, Gratitude, and Love

I would like to thank, first and foremost, all the amazing entities who came to me and allowed me to share their messages and stories here for you to read. I could not have done this without you and I am grateful for the ways in which you have changed my life for the better. You truly make this world a beautiful place.

I would also like to thank my family – my soft and cuddly calico girls who give me the space and fur-free moments to do what I need to do, but also remind me that there's always time for fun, laughter and cuddling; to my fabulous parents, Claudia and Dave, Jim and Cena, for making me who I am in more ways than one and always encouraging me to become something greater; my sister, Stacie and her family of five – Scott, Cody, Megan and Beaux – you all lighten my world with your laughter and grace. I can feel your hugs no matter where we all are on this earth.

To my friends who are my chosen family, my familiars and loves, spread all around this beautiful globe – Elysia, Cassie, and Rob; Hannah, Jason, and the boys; Lune and Seth – each of you has contributed in an unique and important way, helping me create who I am in this world and encouraging me to share it.

And to many friends and extended family who have come before or are still with me though far apart in distance, I am grateful for the many colorful tidings you have shared with me in this life because your beauty has helped me become a greater expression of who I am now.

A lot of heartfelt gratitude goes out to Cheryl and Higgins for waking me up to something new that really changed my life and began this work you are now holding in your hands – your influence and kind words have meant so much to me over the years.

To A.M., the one who sees me through it all, I love you and wouldn't want to do it without you. Ever.

Thank you to Amazon and Angel Girl Publications for making this possible and to so many more individuals out there who also contributed – you've all made a difference and I am grateful for you in my life.

Lastly, but by no means least, I am grateful to you – the one reading this book. Thank you for your decision to expand your awareness and open yourself to the many possibilities our world has to offer. It's an incredible journey and I'm glad we're on it together.

About the Author

Michelle L. Hankes is a practicing intuitive who uses many of the abilities described in this book including clairvoyance, claircognizance, clairaudience, and clairsentience to meet and interact with many different types of physical and non-physical entities. She believes that everyone has these abilities and with a little practice, they are something anyone can use on a daily basis. She spends most of her time writing and connecting with non-physicals in the physical world and has some future plans up her sleeve to begin her next journey into writing about Archangels. She currently lives in Seattle with two fuzzy and cuddly calico cats and a house full of green things. For more information about the author or to download a free e-book about developing your own abilities, please visit www.michellehankes.com.

May this book find you awakened and inspired,
and uplifted by ALL of those around you.
May all of your connections be Divine.

Best Wishes,
M.H.

16210513R00166

Made in the USA
Charleston, SC
09 December 2012